LIFE OF THE TRAIL 2 HISTORIC HIKES IN
NORTHERN YOHO NATIONAL PARK

LIFE OF THE TRAIL 2 HISTORIC HIKES IN
NORTHERN YOHO NATIONAL PARK

By Emerson Sanford & Janice Sanford Beck

Rocky
Mountain Books
VANCOUVER • VICTORIA • CALGARY

Rocky Mountain Books
#108 – 17665 66A Avenue
Surrey, BC V3S 2A7
www.rmbooks.com

Rocky Mountain Books
PO Box 468
Custer, WA
98240-0468

Library and Archives Canada Cataloguing in Publication

Sanford, Emerson
     Historic hikes in Northern Yoho National Park / Emerson Sanford, Janice Sanford Beck.

(Life of the trail ; 2)
Includes bibliographical references and index.
ISBN 978-1-897522-00-4

     1. Hiking—British Columbia—Yoho National Park—Guidebooks. 2. Yoho National Park (B.C.)—Guidebooks. I. Beck, Janice Sanford, 1975- II. Title. III. Series.
GV199.44.C22B729 2008   796.5109711'68   C2007-907285-2

Library of Congress Control Number: 2007943170

Edited by Meaghan Craven
Proofread by Joe Wilderson
Book and cover design by Chyla Cardinal
Front cover photo by Emerson Sanford
Back cover photo courtesy of The Whyte Museum of the Canadian Rockies Archives (V263/NA71-16)
All interior images supplied by the authors except as otherwise noted

Printed and bound in Hong Kong

Rocky Mountain Books gratefully acknowledges the financial support of the Government of Canada through the Book Publishing Industry Development Program (BPIDP); the Canada Council for the Arts; and the province of British Columbia through the British Columbia Arts Council and the Book Publishing Tax Credit for our publishing activities.

This book has been produced on 100% post-consumer recycled paper, processed chlorine free and printed with vegetable-based dyes.

Good old days on the trail and evenings around the campfire, and when the coffee pot upset just as it was beginning to boil and the sugar and salt got wet, and sometimes the beans went sour and the bacon musty and the wind blew smoke in your eyes, and the ashes and sparks on your blankets, the butt of the biggest bough hit the small of your back, and the mosquitoes almost crowded you out of the tent, and you heard the horse bell getting fainter and fainter, and you knew damn well they would be five miles away in the morning – but just the same, O Lord, how I wish I could live them all over again.

–Tom Wilson, "Memories of Golden Days"[1]

Contents

ACKNOWLEDGEMENTS

The preparation for a book of this type requires the perusal of many secondary sources; during our research we read hundreds of books. The authors of the books we used are acknowledged in the Notes section at the end of this book. Many of the books are still in print and readily available. Others required much diligence on the part of reference librarians to obtain interlibrary loans, and we wish to thank the personnel at the Canmore Public Library, especially Michelle Preston and Hélène Lafontaine, for their assistance. Other books and documents were available only through the Whyte Museum & Archives, and we appreciate the efforts of Lena Goon, Elizabeth Kundert-Cameron, D.L. Cameron, Don Bourdon, and Lisa Christensen for steering us on the right track and obtaining materials and images for us.

The Alpine Club of Canada in Canmore kindly allowed us the use of their collection of the *Canadian Alpine Journal*. Others who provided useful discussion and/or materials during the course of the research were: Ron Tozer, Algonquin Park archivist; Lorna Dishkin of the BC Central Coast Archives; Keith Cole; Rene Morton; Thomas Peterson; David Peyto of Peyto Lake Books; Scott Jevons, GIS Specialist, Government of Alberta; and Rod Wallace and Don Mickle of the National Parks Warden Service.

The authors are indebted to Rosemary Ambrose and Sharon Neville of the Waterloo Region Branch of the Ontario Genealogical Society, who provided the obituary of Katherine Hammond Krug, which led us to her son, John Hammond Krug, who in turn directed us to the John Hammond papers at Mount Allison University. Cheryl Ennals of the Mount Allison Archives and Jane Tisdale of the Owens Art Gallery then provided clippings from the Hammond papers and Rhianna Edwards provided a digital image of Hammond. Lindsay Moir of the Glenbow Museum Library and Jo-Anne Colby of the CPR Archives were also helpful in this search.

A large part of the effort in preparing these volumes was in hiking all of the trails and routes described in the history section. Emerson wishes to thank his wife, Cheryl, for the many hours she spent taking him to trailheads and picking him up several days later at a different location, sometimes on remote gravel roads that were not easily accessible. In addition, Cheryl always had in hand a copy of the itinerary for the hike in order to contact the Warden Service if the solo hiker did not emerge from the wilderness at the appointed time (he always did).

In addition, Emerson wishes to acknowledge the many hikers on remote backcountry trails who stopped to chat and made the solitary hikes more enjoyable. Many of these people are mentioned in the text. Others who did not get mentioned were on trails near Lake Minnewanka, Athabasca Pass, Wildflower Creek valley, the Jasper Park North and South Boundary, Job Pass, the Rockwall, and undoubtedly others. There were also several wardens who contributed to the enjoyment of the backcountry experience.

For Janice, this project has been a labour of love, squeezed in amongst various family, community, and work responsibilities. She would like to thank her partner, Shawn, and children, Rowan and Christopher, for their willingness to accommodate the time required for a project of this magnitude. She would also like to thank her parents for sharing their love of history and introducing her to the trails these volumes bring to life.

Finally, the authors would like to express their appreciation to Don Gorman, Meaghan Craven, Chyla Cardinal, and others at Rocky Mountain Books for their efforts in bringing this work from manuscript to publication.

INTRODUCTION

The term "pleasure travel" has always held a certain ambiguity in the Canadian Rockies. The challenges Tom Wilson relates are but a few of the many discomforts to be encountered on the trail. And yet the joys are indescribable. Since time unknown, people have been unable to resist the mountains' call.

The earliest travel through the Rockies was motivated by economic needs. Archaeological evidence indicates that Aboriginal peoples inhabiting the plains and western Rockies traded extensively, most likely establishing many of today's trails through the mountains. Peoples of the foothills also entered the Rockies to hunt the extensive game that made its home there. However, since details of these journeys have not been recorded, very little is known of indigenous peoples' exact routes and destinations.

The second phase of Rocky Mountain exploration was also driven by economic motives – this time those of the European fur trade. Traders, such as David Thompson, some of whose adventures are described in this volume, were often accompanied by Aboriginal guides whose ancestors had been travelling the trails for centuries. Given that the traders' chief objective was to reach the West Coast, they conducted little exploration within the mountains. They simply wanted to find a way through. The earliest fur-trade route across the Rockies – Howse Pass – is described in the first section of this volume.

In a third stage of mountain exploration and travel, between 1858, when the British government sent the Palliser Expedition to gather as much information as possible about the West, and 1885, when the Canadian Pacific Railway (CPR) was completed, mountain travellers continued to focus on finding the most expedient route to the Pacific. In this volume, we will see Dr. James Hector explore Howse Pass on Palliser's behalf and Walter Moberly scout out the region for the CPR.

However, the bulk of the activity described in the following pages took place during the fourth period of Rocky Mountain exploration. The railway's completion allowed a whole new level of access to the Rockies, enabling pleasure-seeking explorers and mountaineers to delve into the region's picturesque valleys and climb what were previously extremely inaccessible peaks. This was the era of the pack train, when outfitters assembled a team of horses and men to guide adventurers wherever their hearts might desire to go.

It was during this period that trails through the mountains began to assume the form we recognize today. Eager to increase tourist traffic, the CPR began cutting recreational trails near the railway. Wealthier patrons' guides began clearing those farther afield and timber cullers cut even more of them to access the forests.

The seed of today's Banff National Park was planted with the establishment of the Banff Hot Springs Reserve in 1885, and it expanded to become Rocky Mountains Park in 1887. Protected areas were also set aside at Glacier and Yoho in 1886; Waterton Lakes and Jasper followed in 1895 and 1907. In 1909 Rocky Mountains Park hired fire and game guardians to enforce park regulations and decided that a network of trails would facilitate this task. By 1914 wardens were regularly patrolling some sixty trails through the park. Some of the non-historic trails likely evolved during this period, as wardens strayed from the establish trails to explore side valleys within their territories.

A new form of backcountry travel also emerged during this fourth period: the escorted outfitted trip. These trips offered the opportunity for large groups of people who did not previously know one another to travel through the mountains with a knowledgeable guide. The two most famous examples, Caroline Hinman's Off the Beaten Track tours and John Murray Gibbon's Trail Riders of the Canadian Rockies, both took advantage of the delightful scenery in the region described in this volume.

It was not long, however, before increasing automobile use and the advent of lightweight camping gear displaced outfitters, guides, and pack trains. By the mid-1930s, alpine adventurers had ready access to well-established trails and could carry on their backs all they needed to survive for two weeks. By this time, virtually all of today's trails through the Rockies had been established except for the inevitable realignments or replacements of existing trails for environmental reasons.

This series will guide readers in early explorers' footsteps along historic mountain routes. The routes have been divided into regions based on the geographical boundaries that influenced nineteenth-century travellers; within each region, routes are presented in order of first use. *Life of the Trail 1* covers trails in the area bounded by the North Saskatchewan River on the north and the Mistaya River, Bow River, and Lake Minnewanka on the west and south. For today's travellers, the area is perhaps more easily defined by the David Thompson Highway (#11) in the north and the Icefields Parkway (#93), the Bow Valley Parkway (#1A), and Lake Minnewanka on the west and south. The most historically significant trip in this area was David Thompson's journey along the Red Deer River to meet a group of Kootenay Indians and take them back to Rocky Mountain House. Later, the Native route over Pipestone Pass to the Kootenay Plains was used extensively by tourist-explorers and mountaineers.

This volume presents the area surrounded by the Kicking Horse River to the south; the Columbia Icefield to the north; and the Bow, Mistaya, and North Saskatchewan rivers to the east. Or, for today's travellers, the Trans-Canada Highway to the south and the Icefields Parkway to the east. In addition to the Howse Pass fur-trade route, this volume describes the adventures of later explorers, who created a popular return trip from the Kootenay Plains by exploring and thereby making accessible the old Native trail down the Amiskwi River. Journeys through the Yoho Valley and Castleguard Meadows make up Routes II and III of this volume.

By reading this book, today's hikers and armchair adventurers will gain an understanding of how early routes through the Rockies were established and what adventures have taken place along them. With a little imagination, readers can envision Jimmy Simpson guiding the very first pack train across the Saskatchewan Glacier or the Walcott family hauling tonnes of priceless fossils from their Burgess Shale quarry (now called the Walcott Quarry). From the comfort of their homes, readers will join mountaineers in seeking out the base of their coveted peaks and artists questing after the perfect view.

As a reader, you will also gain the information you need to follow in their footsteps. Over the years, we the authors have hiked many of these trails together. In the early twenty-first century, Emerson rehiked each and every one of them to ensure the most accurate trail information possible. We provide a general description of the trail – including sights to watch for and hazards to beware of – and share a few stories from our own adventures along the route. When we use the first person "I" in the book regarding adventures along the trails, we are referring to Emerson and his experiences. We have also included a complete trail guide for all routes, including those that do not fall within park boundaries, and have marked the trails on topographic maps.

We hope that through these narratives, hikers and armchair travellers alike will join J. Monroe Thorington in feeling:

> At last there was nothing to do but go; and go we did, into that wondrous land of far-off valleys where the great rivers of a Continent come leaping down in little brooks and arching waterfalls from the ice-tongues; where rise, beyond the old horizon, the castellated crags and snowy spires we had read and dreamed of…. We were not pioneers ourselves, but we journeyed over old trails that were new to us, and with hearts open. Who shall distinguish?[2]

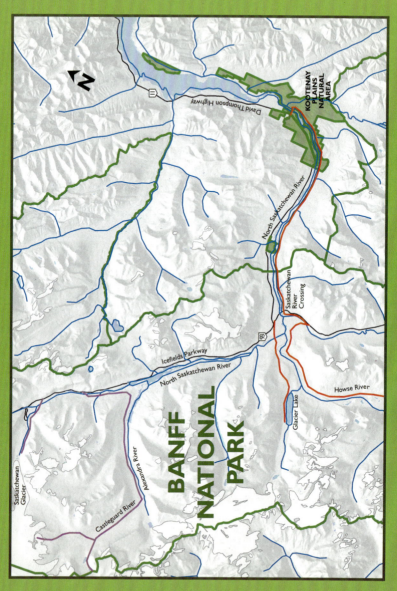

The northern portion of the area west of the Icefields Parkway between the Kicking Horse River and the Columbia Icefield.

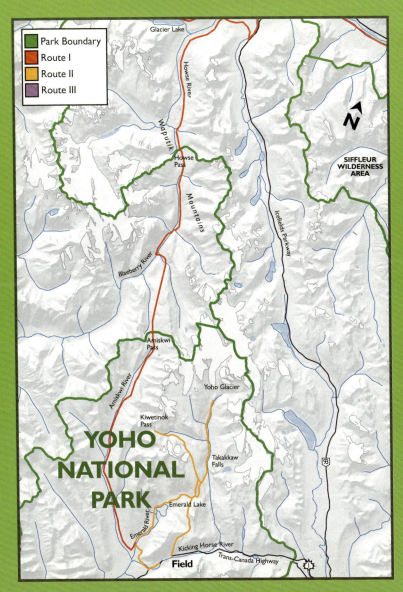

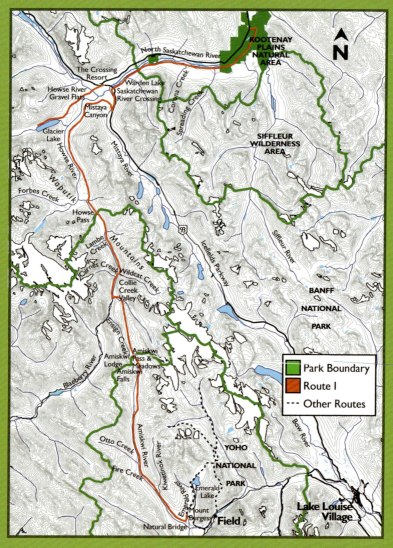

Route 1 from the Kootenay Plains to Field over Howse and Amiskwi passes.

ROUTE I

*Passage to the Coast: David Thompson's and J. Norman Collie's Route
from the Kootenay Plains to Field*

The challenging trail from the southern base of Howse Pass down the Blaeberry River and up the steep ridge to the headwaters of Ensign Creek provoked considerable grief among early travellers. It is now a logging road, suitable for use by ordinary vehicles. For the backpacker, it is a long and dusty slog on a hot day, as there is little protection from the unrelenting rays of the sun.

I managed to beg a ride down the Blaeberry River from the owner of the Mistaya Lodge, high in the Wildcat valley, east of the north end of the logging road. At the junction of the Ensign Creek road, I started walking, steadily making my way around one switchback after another toward the top of the ridge.

About three-quarters of the way up, I began looking for a place to camp. It was late afternoon and I had not seen a good source of water for some time. A beacon of hope descended the hill in the form of men on quads. I stopped one to inquire whether there were any streams coming up near the road. He assured me there were but did not offer to turn around and take me to one. I continued on.

Soon a small pickup truck approached. I took off my pack and stood by the side of the road. The vehicle stopped when it reached me. It was occupied by three middle-aged women. I could see immediately that they were heavily loaded with packs and gear and that although the small truck had a double cab, they were crowded. After chatting for a bit, I told them I had planned to ask them for a ride to the Amiskwi Pass parking lot, but seeing as they had little room, I would continue walking. They readily agreed that they had little extra space but seemed reluctant to drive off. I returned to my pack and prepared to get underway. Still the truck had not left. I started up the road, but I was not alone for long. Being true backcountry travellers, the women caught up with me, stopped, and said that with a little rearranging they should be able to accommodate me.

The three women had been friends for many years, and once a year, if possible, they liked to leave family behind and have some "bonding time" in the backcountry. They were very elusive about exactly where they were going, probably wanting to ensure that they would not have any visitors. They revealed only that they knew of a little cabin near the pass where they could stay. I knew that the only cabin in the area was the warden cabin but did not reveal this information. I was very appreciative of the ride and did not intend to intrude on their solitude.

My only objective when we reached the clear-cut at the end of the road was to find some water where I could set up camp. Ensign Creek proved to be only a short distance from our destination and the clear-cut provided the necessary flat space. The three ladies ate their supper in the parking lot and headed on their way. The next morning I crossed Amiskwi Pass and walked past the warden cabin, some distance away. True to my expectation, I could see the three backcountry friends moving about the cabin.

CHRONOLOGY

−1800   The route over Amiskwi and Howse passes is part of the old Kootenay Trail, used for many years prior to the arrival of Europeans.

1800   Fur traders La Gasse and Le Blanc leave Rocky Mountain House with a Kootenay band and become the first recorded white men to cross Howse Pass.

1801   "The Rook" leads James Hughes, David Thompson, and a group of North West Company (NWC) employees and their families on an abortive trip along the North Saskatchewan and Ram rivers, looking for a passage across the mountains.

1802   Duncan McGillivray leaves Rocky Mountain House due to illness. David Thompson is reassigned to the Peace River country.

1806   David Thompson returns to Rocky Mountain House and prepares for a trip across the mountains.

In the fall, Thompson sends Jaco Findlay and three men to cut a trail over Howse Pass and down the Blaeberry to the Columbia River, thus creating the first man-made trail across the Rockies.

1807   On May 10, a large party led by David Thompson leaves Rocky Mountain House by canoe and horseback, following Jaco Findlay's trail to Howse Pass.

In early June, David Thompson and his men camp on the gravel flats of the Howse River waiting for the snow to melt on the pass. Thompson follows a fast-moving stream flowing into the Howse River and discovers Glacier Lake.

On June 22, Thompson and Bercier advance toward the height of land and cross Howse Pass. Two days later, the entire party follows and sets up camp on the first white man's pass across the Rockies.

1809   Joseph Howse crosses Howse Pass. The pass is named after him.

In 1957 the Canadian government honoured David Thompson, Canada's great surveyor and map-maker, by by depicting his image on a postage stamp.

1810   David Thompson's fall attempt to cross Howse Pass is blocked by Peigans.

1811   Alexander Henry (the younger) sets out from Rocky Mountain House in February with two men and three dog sleds. They successfully evade the Peigans and make the last fur-trade crossing of Howse Pass. The trail returns to its natural state.

1858   Dr. James Hector proceeds north along the North Saskatchewan River with Native guides Nimrod and William. They rediscover and name Glacier Lake. They reach Thompson's camping spot on the gravel flats, but the season is too late for them to proceed toward the pass.

1859   After being deserted by his guides, Hector leads his party across Howse Pass. They make their way along the Blaeberry to the Columbia River. No trace of the old fur-trade trail remains.

1871   Late in the fall, Walter Moberly leads a survey party to the Columbia at the mouth of the Blaeberry River and cuts a trail to the top of Howse Pass. The workers are pushed back by winter weather, but Moberly manages to cross the pass and continue on to the Kootenay Plains. He recommends the pass as a route for the Canadian Pacific Railway (CPR).

1872   Howse Pass is abandoned as a route for the transcontinental railway.

1882   Tom Wilson crosses Howse Pass and laboriously makes his way down the Blaeberry on behalf of Major A.B. Rogers. He reports unfavourably on the Blaeberry River as a possible route for the railway.

1887   Tom Wilson takes a hunting party over Howse Pass but has to abandon his horses along the Blaeberry because he cannot get through the tangle of fallen trees.

1897   Bill Peyto guides J. Norman Collie and G.P. Baker over Howse Pass. They start down the Blaeberry, only to be stopped by fallen timber. As a result, they rediscover the old Native route over Amiskwi Pass and on to the Kicking Horse River.

1898   Peyto leads Walter Wilcox over Howse Pass and on to Amiskwi Pass, which they cross in a snowstorm late in October.

1901   Edward Whymper and Rev. James Outram travel north along the Amiskwi River as far as the mouth of the Kiwetinok River.

1906   Billy Warren guides Mary Schäffer across Amiskwi Pass from the south. They proceed over Howse Pass to the Kootenay Plains before returning by the same route.

1906   The Bella Coola and Fraser Lake Railway proposes to build a railway from Red Deer to the Pacific Ocean at Bella Coola & Fraser over Howse Pass and down the Blaeberry River. The line is never built.

1910   J.E.C. Eaton follows Schäffer's lead, crossing Amiskwi and Howse passes from the south.

1917   R.W. Cautley and A.O. Wheeler lead the Boundary Commission survey along the Continental Divide in the Howse Pass area.

1919   Dr. Charles Walcott and Mary Vaux Walcott spend a month collecting fossils and studying geology in the Glacier Lake area.

1920   J.W.A. Hickson uses the Howse/Amiskwi passes route to spend a month climbing around the Columbia Icefields area.

1922   J. Monroe Thorington and friends cross Amiskwi and Howse passes to the Howse River area.

1923   Seventeen members of the Appalachian Mountaineering Club make their way over Amiskwi Pass and along the flooded Blaeberry River to Howse Pass and the North Saskatchewan River.

1924   Caroline Hinman guides one of her Off the Beaten Track tours from the Kicking Horse River over Amiskwi and Howse passes and on to the Saskatchewan River. The party of twenty-three spends three days camping on top of historic Howse Pass.

1928   Caroline Hinman and her Off the Beaten Track tour use the same route to return home from a long trip to the north. They spend the last night of their tour in the luxury of the Emerald Lake cabins.

History

First Peoples

Archaeological evidence indicates that both Plains and Plateau peoples spent time in the North Saskatchewan River/Howse Pass region of Banff National Park.[1] Farther west, the river valleys of what is now Yoho National Park appear to have housed stopover camps used for buffalo hide preparation and meat drying. Campsites near the mouth of the Amiskwi River date back to 1800, soon after Europeans had arrived in the area.

One of the routes the Plains and Plateau peoples frequently trod was between the ochre beds near Vermilion Pass (in what is today Kootenay National Park) and the Kootenay Plains. They followed today's Amiskwi River to the pass, travelled along part of the Blaeberry River to Howse Pass, and then traced the Howse and Saskatchewan rivers to the Kootenay Plains.

Little did they know that new connections were about to change their lives dramatically.

A moose drinks at a mineral lick near the mouth of the Amiskwi River. Two hundred years ago, Aboriginal people travelling from the Paint Pots to the Kootenay Plains likely camped nearby.

Fur Traders

It was June 22, 1807. For two weeks the gravel flats of the west branch of
the Saskatchewan (Howse) River had been occupied by four fur traders,
heralds of events to come. As one of them, David Thompson,[2] recorded
in his journal:

> Here among ... [the mountains'] stupendous and solitary
> wilds covered with eternal Snow, and Mountain connected
> with Mountain by immense Glaciers, the collection of
> Ages and on which the Beams of the Sun makes hardly
> any Impression when aided by the most favourable
> weather, I stayed for fourteen days more, impatiently
> waiting the melting of the Snows on the Height of Land
> [Howse Pass].[3]

Thompson was a man with a mission, and his patience was running
low. Seven years had passed since the North West Company (NWC
or Nor'Westers) had first posted him to Rocky Mountain House, a
fort in the eastern foothills. He had been assigned to assist Duncan
McGillivray in leading an expedition across the mountains the
following spring. Late that fall, Thompson and his men entered the
mountains along the Red Deer River to meet a band of Kootenay
Indians and lead them back to the fort.[4]

When the Kootenays returned home, Thompson sent two trappers
and traders, Charles La Gasse and Pierre Le Blanc, to accompany them.
Determined to avoid the harassment they had experienced from the
Peigans on the way east, the band followed the North Saskatchewan and
Howse rivers to Howse Pass. As a result, La Gasse and Le Blanc became
the first recorded white men to cross Howse Pass. Returning east at the
end of May 1801, the two men brought furs – both trapped and traded
with the Kootenays – and important information about the land across
the mountains.

McGillivray was more anxious than ever to launch his delayed
expedition, but the guide the Kootenay chiefs sent to lead the
Nor'Westers across the mountains had been killed by a group of Stoneys

along the way. Undeterred, McGillivray hired a Cree known as "the Rook" who claimed to know a good horse trail across the mountains. Thompson had great misgivings about "the Rook," declaring him "a Man so timourous by Nature, of so wavering a Disposition, & withal so addicted to flattering & lying, as to make every Thing he said or did, equivocal and doubtful."[5]

When the time came to leave, McGillivray was too ill to accompany the group. He appointed James Hughes, proprietor of Rocky Mountain House, as the leader. On June 6, 1801, the party headed west along the North Saskatchewan River toward Howse Pass and the Pacific Ocean. Included among the party were "the Rook" and his wife, Hughes, Thompson, nine Nor'Westers, and thirteen horses loaded with trade goods and other necessities.

The trip was plagued with difficulties from the beginning. As Thompson had suspected, "the Rook" did not know the way. He led the adventurers up the Ram River to a dead end at its headwaters. The trip was a total failure and the disconsolate party returned to Rocky Mountain House. As Thompson reported to McGillivray, "How unfortunate has this Journey been from the beginning, when we had got all ready & waited a long Time! At length a Kootanae came to guide us, & he when within a few miles of the fort was murdered."[6]

Thompson's journals do not reveal why the two traders, La Gasse and Le Blanc, who had just returned from across the mountains, were not asked to guide the expedition. In fact, La Gasse and Le Blanc appeared to have disappeared entirely from fur-trade history until anthropologist Claude Schaeffer's 1965 interview with elders of the Tobacco Plains Kootenai people.[7] As the elders' story of the first white men in the memory of their tribe progressed, it became obvious to Schaeffer that its subjects were La Gasse and Le Blanc, who would likely have wintered with a Tobacco Plains band in 1800.

The elders explained that in the summer or fall of 1801, the two trappers returned across the mountains to the Tobacco Plains and one of them married a daughter of the chief. Each spring for either three or five years, the trappers continued to cross the mountains with the winter's furs. On the last of these trips, the two traders, the Kootenai wife, and the couple's infant son were confronted by a band of Stoneys. The band demanded that the traders reveal where they were coming from and who their guide was. La Gasse and Le Blanc replied that the guide, who was in fact a son of the chief, hailed from an eastern tribe. Trusting that they had successfully deceived the Stoneys, they continued on their way.

But the Stoneys suspected the truth. They followed the traders' tracks back to the Kootenai camp. Finding that the men were out hunting, they attacked and killed many of the women and children. The chief and his hunters returned to a scene of terrible carnage. Incensed, the chief concluded that his white guests had betrayed him by deliberately revealing the camp's location.

When La Gasse and Le Blanc returned that fall, he promptly killed them both. In fact, so great was his fury that only his daughter's intervention prevented him from taking the life of his infant grandson. Eventually, his son did manage to convince him that the two white men were blameless, but it was, of course, too late. And thus the fate of the first white men to cross Howse Pass passed into Kootenai tribal lore.[8]

Meanwhile, priorities were changing at Nor'Wester headquarters. The spring of 1802 saw McGillivray's continuing illness cause him to leave the West. Thompson accepted an assignment to a post in the Peace River country, and the fort at Rocky Mountain House shut down. But Howse Pass was not to remain protected from trans-Atlantic trade needs for long. By 1806 North West Company officials had revived their interest in developing a navigable route through the mountains that would extend trade to the Pacific Coast. Thompson was assigned to the task. He returned to Rocky Mountain House in the fall of 1806 to prepare for a spring crossing.

Thompson's first step was to send his assistant, Jacques Raphael (Jaco) Findlay; a fellow named McMaster; and two of his men, Boulard and Bercier, to cut a trail suitable for pack horses. They were to follow the Kootenay route up the Saskatchewan and Howse rivers to the pass, chop a trail down the Blaeberry River, and build canoes at its junction with the Columbia (which Thompson believed to be the Kootenay). Findlay returned to Rocky Mountain House in November with a report and a hand-drawn map. He and his assistants had cut the first man-made trail across the Rockies.

While Findlay and his men cleared the trail, another obstacle to Thompson's journey conveniently cleared itself. With good reason, Thompson had been quite concerned about Peigan hostility toward Europeans trading with their enemies, the Kootenays. The Lewis and Clark expedition, which was crossing the continent farther south, inadvertently solved the problem for him. Members of the expedition had been in a skirmish with a Native band and had killed one of its members. The Peigans headed south to help their neighbours avenge the killing, leaving Thompson free to head west without any trouble.

Preparations continued over the winter, with Thompson arranging for more than a thousand pounds (454 kilograms) of supplies to be transported up the Saskatchewan River by dogsled. On May 4, 1807, the river ice broke up and the Nor'Westers started packing. On May 10, Finan McDonald, Thompson's clerk and deputy, and five voyageurs (Boisverd, Lussier, Le Camble, Beaulieu, and Buche) began paddling up the North Saskatchewan River. Meanwhile, Thompson followed a parallel route along the river with his wife, Charlotte, and their three small children; Lussier's family; another woman; three of Thompson's men: Clément, Bercier, and Boulard; and a string of pack horses. All told, there were close to thirty horses, four men, three women, and eight or nine children.

By June 3, the overland contingent had caught up with McDonald's party at the Kootenay Plains. After resting the horses for two days, Thompson and his three men continued on horseback and the voyageurs continued by canoe, leaving the women, children, and pack horses in the care of Finan McDonald at "... the last & only Place, where Pasture could be found for the Horses, or animals for the People for Food."[9]

It is here, on the Kootenay Plains,[10] that today's trail over Howse Pass begins. It is still a popular camping and resting spot for many people.

Both the riders and the voyageurs carried on until they reached the gravel flats of the Howse River, where the water became too shallow for the canoes to proceed and the snow too deep for the horses. It was there that Thompson set up camp and sent all but the three men travelling with him back to the Kootenay Plains to wait for the snow to melt. On the gravel flats, Thompson's men occupied themselves by splitting logs into boards and making boxes for their trade goods.

One day, Thompson followed a fast-moving stream that flowed into the Howse River from a side valley to the northwest. He discovered it to be the outflow from a large and beautiful lake surrounded by mountains, and he marvelled that the peaks at the end of the lake all seemed to be covered in glaciers. Fifty-one years later, the Palliser Expedition's Dr. James Hector would camp on the shores of this same lake and name it Glacier Lake (see page 33).

Right: Today's trail along the North Saskatchewan River is used for many purposes. This viewing platform is likely used by hunters and wildlife watchers for observing game.

Opposite: A structure along the North Saskatchewan River trail, likely an old food cache. Early travellers would have used such structures to protect food reserves from wild animals.

By June 22 spring had finally advanced far enough for Thompson and Bercier to attempt the pass. Nearly seven years after Thompson had first been sent to the area, he was at last to glimpse the western valley. By mid-morning, the two men had reached the broad, flat meadow that constitutes the pass and found spring water and melting snow flowing west. Thompson "paused to pray to the Lord: 'May God in his Mercy give us to see where it's waters flow into the Ocean, & return in safety."[11] Two days later, the entire party had assembled near Thompson's campsite to finish packing. What could not be carried was left with McDonald until the men could return for it. Nearly thirty horses carried the large group westward early the next morning. Even travelling slowly, they had reached the Continental Divide (Thompson's and Bercier's pass), by early afternoon.

They proceeded to pitch camp on the summit of the first white man's pass across the Rockies south of the Peace River district. It was spring on the western side of the Rockies and the melting snow made what is now called the Blaeberry River deep and fast. Though waiting for the snow to melt had required much patience, it was nothing in comparison with the challenges yet to be endured en route to the Columbia. As Thompson explained: "The water descending in innumerable Rills, soon swelled

Above: The gravel flats of the Howse River where David Thompson set up camp in the spring of 1807.

Opposite: Today's summit marker on the top of Howse Pass.

our Brook to a Rivulet, with a Current foaming white, the Horses with Difficulty crossed & recrossed at every 2 or 300 yards, & the men crossed by clinging to the Tails & Manes of the Horses, & yet ran no small Danger of being swept away & drowned."[12]

After a very difficult week crossing and recrossing the Blaeberry River and chopping their way through thick forest, Thompson's party reached the Columbia. The quality of Jaco Findlay's trail left much to be desired, but they were grateful for the satisfactory map he had drawn. Now that the route was better established, four men and twelve pack horses headed back across the mountains to fetch Finan McDonald and the remainder of the supplies. This part of the group returned on July 12, allowing the entire party to head upriver toward Lake Windermere.

That fall, McDonald crossed back over Howse Pass with five voyageurs and a load of furs, returning to Thompson's post on Lake Windermere with trade goods by early November. Howse Pass had been successfully adopted as a trade route.

David Thompson's routine of crossing east in the spring with his men and returning west in the fall would continue for several years. He did not, however, bring his family back over the pass – except to return permanently to the east in 1808. In fact, the initial trip over Howse Pass and back marked the first and last time Thompson's family accompanied him on a major journey. His journals do not indicate a specific reason for this exclusion, but the trip down the Blaeberry River would have been enough to deter even the most adventurous of individuals.

The few times Thompson does refer to his family in his journal suggest further reasons. On the return trip in 1808, Thompson notes that the horse carrying Fanny (age seven) and Samuel (age four) tried to buck its load: "One of my horses nearly crushing my children to death from having his load poorly put on, which I mistook for being vicious; I shot him on the spot and rescued my little ones."[13]

Near the top of the pass, another crisis occurred. Little Emma (age two) disappeared and was only found several hours later, nearly a mile (1.6 kilometres) away. The relieved group continued to the Kootenay Plains by horseback and by canoe to Rocky Mountain House without further incident. Nevertheless, the stress of the journey appears to have been such that Thompson's family did not accompany him on any of his later expeditions.

In the fall of 1810, David Thompson was about to cross the pass once again when he found its entrance blocked by Peigans. Little did he know, the Hudson's Bay Company (HBC) had been watching his success in the western fur trade with great interest. They had sent Joseph Howse on an exploratory trip to the mountains in 1809 and followed it up with a trade excursion over Howse Pass the next summer. The Peigans had grown increasingly disturbed

by the Europeans trading with their enemies across the mountains. Howse managed to slip past them along the Saskatchewan River but found them waiting for him across the pass.

He and his companions, the first HBC men to cross the mountains, were warned that if they crossed the pass again, they would be brutally killed. In spite of a very successful trade that winter, which resulted in thirty-six bundles of fur being brought east over the pass in the spring of 1811, Howse gave up the any further thoughts of establishing trade across the mountains. Ironically, the pass was eventually named after him.[14] Meanwhile Thompson laboriously made his way north, eventually crossing the mountains over Athabasca Pass.

The 1810 Peigan blockade effectively ended the use of Howse Pass as a fur-trade route. However, thanks to a combination of deceit and skilful manoeuvring, one final trip was completed. Alexander Henry (the younger) had arrived at Rocky Mountain House on October 5, 1810, in time to assist Thompson with his trip north toward Athabasca Pass. On February 3, he, two other men, and three dog sledges set out with supplies for Thompson.

With the Peigans closely watching any movements from the fort, Henry informed them his party was headed downstream to another fur-trading post. They travelled one mile (1.6 kilometres), circled back through the woods behind the fort, and proceeded upriver on the ice. On February 9, a couple of days' journey past the Kootenay Plains, they abandoned the sledges and continued to the top of Howse Pass on snowshoes. From there, Henry sent the men and supplies on to Kootenay House while he returned to the Kootenay Plains on his own. By February 13, Henry was back at Rocky Mountain House, having concluded his only trip to the mountains and the last fur-trade expedition over Howse Pass.[15] The trail over the pass and down the Blaeberry was allowed to return to its natural state.

PALLISER EXPEDITION

Nearly half a century passed before the third period of exploration brought European men back to Howse Pass. In 1857 Captain John Palliser was commissioned to spend three years exploring the land west of present-day Manitoba. He assigned the area north of the Bow River to Dr. James Hector,[16] mandating him to explore the region between the Bow River and Athabasca Pass. Having just survived the incident that gave Kicking Horse Pass its name in his effort to complete a circuit over Vermilion Pass and back to the Bow Valley Hector[17] hoped to explore David Thompson's Howse Pass before retreating to winter quarters at Edmonton House.

On September 8, 1858, Hector and his Aboriginal guides and helpers, Peter Erasmus, Nimrod, Sutherland, and Brown proceeded north along the Bow River, over Bow Summit, and down the Mistaya River to the North Saskatchewan. In so doing, Hector became the first recorded European to cross from the headwaters of the Bow to the North Saskatchewan along a route that would become world famous.

Hector did not have a copy of either the map drawn by Jaco Findlay or Thompson's later version, and his guides were not familiar with the route to Howse Pass. They set out west from the Saskatchewan River through heavy forest, arriving at Thompson's beautiful lake on September 11. Hector named it Glacier Lake and moved camp to the base of the glacier. On September 13, he and his assistant, Sutherland, explored the glacier, which Hector named Lyell Glacier after the distinguished British geologist Sir Charles Lyell. He also named the high point at the centre of the glacier Mount Lyell.[18]

Although winter was fast approaching, Hector continued exploring long enough to find the spot on the Howse River gravel flats where Thompson had camped some fifty-one years previously. But with the snow that blocked Thompson's journey threatening to overtake him as well, Hector could not afford to tarry. Had he realized he was only a few hours from the top of the pass, he might have persisted. Instead, he allowed the lateness of the season to press him toward Fort Edmonton without having attained his goal.

David Thompson first viewed Glacier Lake while waiting for the snow to melt on Howse Pass in the spring of 1807. Dr. James Hector named it fifty-one years later.

The following autumn, Hector and his guides again prepared to cross Howse Pass. This time, rather than going up the Bow River, William suggested a route over Pipestone Pass to the North Saskatchewan River.[19] There, in spite of their earlier promise to accompany Hector as far as the top of Howse Pass, the guides unexpectedly deserted. Hector's party now consisted of himself, four men, five saddle horses, and eight pack horses. He found that:

> … my duty was to go before and act as guide; so that I was now not only the directing, but also the actual explorer of the country; and it needed all the little experience I had picked up of the Indian's tact in threading through forest country in a given direction: and I daresay that, without knowing it, we often followed a roundabout and bad line of route, when a better [one] existed.[20]

They easily found their way to the spot on the Howse River gravel flats where Hector had been the year before. From there, he led them up a valley that proved to be blocked by today's Freshfield Glacier. Retreating to the Howse River, they managed to follow it to the top of the pass. With considerable difficulty, the party then followed the Blaeberry River toward the Columbia. The route was severely obstructed by fallen timber. Hector found no indication of recent use of the trail and hardly any trace of the old fur-trade trail. Still, his party managed to reach the Columbia on September 17 and eventually make its way to Lake Windermere and along the old fur-trade route to the Pacific.

RAILWAY SURVEYORS

After two years of hard work, members of the Palliser Expedition had explored four passes through the Rockies previously known to Europeans: the North Kootenay, the Kananaskis, the Vermilion, and the Howse (see pages 33). They had also discovered another pass: the Kicking Horse. In Victoria in the fall of 1859, Palliser and Hector met with Walter Moberly, a man obsessed with finding a route for the railway through the Rockies. Their message was very discouraging to a railway man: they did not believe there was any possibility of running a transcontinental railway through Canadian territory.[21]

Twelve years later, British Columbia had joined Confederation, the Canadian government had committed to building a national railway and Sir Sandford Fleming had been put in charge of surveys to determine a route. Walter Moberly was tasked with finding a way through the Rockies. He instructed party "S" to survey Howse Pass, which, in spite of Hector's misgivings, he believed to be the best route. Where previous explorers had made their initial approach from the east, party "S" – with their forty-five pack animals carrying seven tons (6,350 kilograms) of food and equipment – set out from the west coast.[22]

After two and a half months of very strenuous work, the four surveyors, sixteen men (mainly axemen), eight packers, and one hunter reached the mouth of the Blaeberry River on the Columbia. Due to a late start and lengthy journey, it was October 3, 1871, before they reached this point, and snow was already falling on the high mountain peaks. After an uncomfortable night on boggy ground, the party retreated a few miles south to a better camping spot (today's Bergenham Wildlife Sanctuary), which would become the beginning of the trail toward Howse Pass.

Thompson and his men had travelled the route laden with bulky furs. Hector had assessed its feasibility for grander transportation schemes, and now Moberly's surveyors were to investigate further. Twelve years of silence was broken by the ringing of axes as the men began the Herculean task of chopping a pathway along the Blaeberry River. The party finally reached the top of Howse Pass, covering a distance of approximately forty miles (sixty-four kilometres), on October 26. The surveyors were keen to begin their all-important task, but snow had already begun to drift down from the sky. To add to the dusting, eight inches (twenty centimetres) fell the following day, then another twelve (thirty centimetres). There was no choice but to settle in for the long winter.[23]

Moberly set the men to work building log huts at the depot on the Columbia, near the beginning of the newly cut trail. The mountain trails would not be passable again until May, and it would be June before pack horses could safely be taken over the pass. Twenty-nine members of the party, including two ex-convicts, would be confined in very cramped quarters for the next six or seven months.

Anxious to see if his chosen route was indeed suitable for building a railway, Walter Moberly pushed ahead of the main party. He had left the Columbia on October 10 in order to assess the terrain for grades and reached the top of the pass about five days later. He does not comment on any undue difficulty crossing the river or navigating fallen trees, though his slow pace suggests the going was not entirely smooth.

Afraid of being trapped by winter weather, his Native guides and packers wanted to turn back at the top of the pass. But Moberly was determined to carry on. Three days later they were at the Kootenay Plains. Moberly was now absolutely convinced that this was the route for the railway,[24] "satisfied that the whole difficulty in this route is from the Divide westerly for eight to ten miles [sixteen kilometres] down Blueberry River."[25]

On October 21, Moberly hurried back over Howse Pass to rejoin his men. He did not spend the winter with them but left on December 4 to make an amazing mid-winter journey across the Selkirks and on to Victoria. In June 1872, he returned to the site near the mouth of the Blaeberry River with discouraging news: the Howse Pass route had been abandoned. His team was instructed to move up the Columbia to Athabasca Pass, then on to the Yellowhead Pass, which had been chosen as the new route for the railway.

By the summer of 1881, the railway engineers had again changed their minds. Major A.B. Rogers, engineer-in-charge of the mountain section of the Canadian Pacific Railway, had discovered today's Rogers Pass through the Selkirk Mountains and by the end of 1881 had decided to use Kicking Horse Pass to get through the Rockies. However, Major Rogers had never been over Howse Pass, and was having second thoughts about Kicking Horse Pass. He decided to investigate the route himself.

The spring of 1882 saw Rogers start up the Bow River with a young Tom Wilson as assistant. Progress up the Bow and down the Mistaya to the Howse River was slower than anticipated. Anxious about the duties he was neglecting while on the trail, the major convinced Wilson to take enough food for ten days and carry on alone by foot. The major would cross Kicking Horse Pass and meet him at

Walter Moberly, seventh from the left, in a party of CPR surveyors. Moberly was convinced that Howse Pass was the best route for the railway.

the mouth of the Blaeberry River in ten days, with a nice bonus for the adventuresome worker.

In spite of the considerable traffic it had seen, the route was much more difficult than Wilson had anticipated. "When I began the real descent of Howse pass it was even more difficult than the Kicking Horse," he later explained. "There were times when I could not travel a mile [1.6 kilometres] in an hour."[26] Thirteen days passed before an extremely tired and hungry explorer met up with Rogers at the mouth of the Blaeberry. The trail Moberly's men had cut eleven years earlier must have been obscured by fallen trees; nature reclaims its own very quickly in the mountains' dense coniferous forest. Tom Wilson's report on the potential of Howse Pass for the railway convinced Major Rogers of the soundness of his original decision, and the railway was subsequently built through Kicking Horse Pass.

This was not to be Wilson's last encounter with the Blaeberry. Five years later, having quit his job with the railway and gone into business as an outfitter, he took his first hunting clients to the area he remembered around the North Saskatchewan and Howse rivers. After the hunt, the customers insisted on returning to the Columbia Valley over Howse Pass and down the Blaeberry. Either Wilson had not learned his lesson or it was a case of "the customer is always right." Regardless, travel was so difficult that they were eventually forced to abandon the horses and complete the journey to the Columbia on foot. With his clients safe and sound in their hotel, Wilson hired axe men to return with him and rescue his horses from the fallen timber.

Major A.B. Rogers, the irascible, tobacco-spitting, foul talking engineer-in-charge of the mountain section for the CPR, was nicknamed Hell's Bells Rogers. He was responsible for discovering Rogers Pass.

THOMAS EDMONDS WILSON (1859–1933)

Tom Wilson, the man who did more than any other to blaze the early trails in the Canadian Rockies, got his start in the Canadian Pacific Railway survey camps. As a young adult, he also spent time trapping and prospecting in the mountains, travelling with Native parties and assisting with the Dominion Topographic Survey. His nearly photographic memory for mountain trails allowed him to retain details of every pass, valley, and lake he viewed. Over a period of twenty years, he outfitted nearly every important exploration party heading into the backcountry. Information from these trips – alongside that from his early travels – made him a virtual encyclopedia of the area.

Wilson was born in Bondhead, north of Toronto, on August 21, 1859. His family moved to Barrie when he was very young. Life on the farm did not suit young Tom, and at the age of sixteen he left to seek adventure elsewhere. Illness forced him home three years later, but he stayed only a year before discovering his ticket west with the North West Mounted Police. He joined in 1888 but soon found that the day-to-day routine of police work did not suit his adventurous spirit. He purchased his discharge on May 16, 1881.

Wilson soon found work with the CPR. He began as a packer, then became personal assistant to surveyor Major Rogers. The two travelled widely together, particularly to the Rocky Mountain survey camps. During his tenure with the railway, Wilson became the first white man to see both Lake Louise and Emerald Lake. He spent his winters trapping or prospecting; it was one of these trips that led him into the Yoho Valley in 1884.

The following year proved to be a significant turning point in Wilson's life. Having joined Major Steele's Scouts, he participated in quelling the Riel Rebellion. He returned just in time to board a train for Craigellachie and witness the driving of the "last spike," signalling the completion of the national railway. Then, on October 19, he married Minnie McDougall, a native of Owen Sound, Ontario, who ran a boarding house with her brother in the short-lived Silver City, located near the base of Castle Mountain. Wilson took over from McDougall; he and Minnie ran the boarding house for a year before leaving for a homestead near Morley in 1886.

It was then that Wilson began the outfitting business that would occupy most of his next eighteen years. Over the years, his outfitting business extended from Banff to Laggan (Lake Louise) and Field; it did not take him long to become the most knowledgeable and respected outfitter in the business. Many future guides, including Bill Peyto and Jimmy Simpson, got their start working for Wilson. In 1893 he moved his family to Banff and was instrumental in starting the Banff Indian Days the following year. He also formed two business partnerships, first with George Fear and his brother William, acquaintances who were original inhabitants of Siding 29

Tom Wilson started his long life in the mountains as a packer and assistant to Major A.B. Rogers. He was the first non-Native to view both Lake Louise and Emerald Lake.

(Banff), and later with Robert Campbell, a schoolteacher who worked as a guide for Wilson during the summers and later became his bookkeeper.

Wilson's life took another turn in 1903 when he established a ranch to winter his horses on the Kootenay Plains. Enjoying life on the Plains, he started a trading post the following year and began spending his winters on the ranch. In 1904 he sold his outfitting business in order to concentrate on the ranch and trading post. Two years later he became a founding member of the Alpine Club of Canada – a fitting act for someone who had helped so many mountaineers reach the base of their chosen peaks.

After nearly losing his life in the mountains three years earlier, he decided to sell the ranch in 1911. By 1921 he had become disillusioned with mountain life. He retired to Enderby, BC. But the call of the mountains proved too strong for him to resist. In 1924 the Trail Riders of the Canadian Rockies acknowledged his considerable contributions to trail life in the Rockies by unveiling a plaque in his honour in the Yoho Valley, which he had explored forty years earlier. In 1927 he returned permanently to Banff.

Wilson's final years were spent entertaining guests at the Banff Springs Hotel. He provided "local colour" by telling stories of his past experiences to tourists and newspaper reporters, and was not averse to embellishing a story to add to its entertainment value. He died in 1933 and is buried in the Old Banff Cemetery, his grave marked with the Yoho Valley plaque.

Amiskwi Pass

Ten years passed before another group is reported to have attempted the Howse Pass route. By then, the railway had been transporting tourists and mountaineers to Banff, Laggan, and Field for more than a decade. Sooner or later, someone was bound to venture over Howse Pass. Finally, in the fall of 1897, mountaineers J. Norman Collie and George P. Baker decided to head north for some climbing and exploration. They hired a Swiss guide, Peter Sarbach, and an outfit from Tom Wilson consisting of Bill Peyto as guide, L. Richardson as packer, and C. Black as cook.

Peter Sarbach standing, George Baker (l), and J. Norman Collie relaxing before a trip. These mountaineers were the first group to attempt the route over Amiskwi Pass.

45

EBENEZER WILLIAM (BILL) PEYTO (1869–1943)

Bill Peyto was born on February 14, 1869, in Kent, England, the third of nine children in a family of very modest means. His upbringing was largely rural and his education took place in the local public school. He learned early in life that success depended on being hard working and self-reliant.

At the age of eighteen, he immigrated to Halifax, Nova Scotia, where he arrived in February 1887. The newly completed Canadian Pacific Railway carried him west toward the Rockies. He spent the next few years working various jobs between Cochrane and Banff, developing a knowledge of geology and palaeontology. Prospecting and trapping contributed to his sustenance. Having developed an intimate knowledge of the mountains, in 1893 or 1894 he fell naturally into employment as one of Tom Wilson's outfitters and guides.

Peyto spent several years with Wilson, during which time he was a highly respected, if somewhat colourful, guide. Climber Walter Wilcox described him as "[assuming] a wild and picturesque though somewhat tattered attire. A sombrero, with a rakish tilt to one side, a blue shirt set off by a white kerchief … and a buckskin coat with fringed border, add to his cowboy appearance. A heavy belt containing a row of cartridges, hunting-knife and six-shooter, as well as the restless activity of his wicked blue eyes, give him an air of bravado."[27]

Wilcox found the guide "very quiet in civilization, but … more communicative around an evening camp-fire." He identified Peyto as "one of the most conscientious and experienced men with horses that I have ever known." And yet, "quick and cool in time of real danger, he has too much anxiety about trouble ahead, and worries himself terribly about imaginary evils. He sleeps with a loaded rifle and a hunting-knife by his side."[28]

Bill Peyto, a colourful, conscientious and highly respected guide, helped pioneer the route over Amiskwi Pass.

In 1900 Peyto left Banff to fight in the Boer War. Upon his return the following year, he began his own outfitting business, and in 1902 he married Emily Wood, the sister of a fellow outfitter. This was undoubtedly the happiest time in Peyto's life. The couple had one son, Robin, before tragedy struck: Emily died of a brain hemorrhage in 1906.

Not only was Peyto devastated by the death of his wife, but his extended sojourns on the trail meant that he also had to give his beloved son to a cousin of Emily's, who agreed to look after him in Armstrong, BC. Abandoning his outfitting business, Peyto spent the next five years hunting, trapping, working his mine, and doing the odd outfitting stint for the Brewsters.

By 1911 his life had stabilized enough that he decided to join the newly formed Warden Service. He stayed until 1915, when he left to join the army. A year later he was wounded in action near Ypres and sent home. He was grateful for the opportunity to spend time with his son, but circumstances were such that he saw little of Robin after that summer. He rejoined the Warden Service in 1920 and within a year had been taken on full time.

The position offered a level of financial stability Peyto had never previously experienced. On November 15, 1921, he married Ethel Wells of Banff. Although the marriage lasted until Ethel died in 1940, they saw little of each other, with Peyto spending most of his time alone at one of his cabins in the Simpson Pass district. As he got older, he became more eccentric, likely at least partly a result of his lonely lifestyle. He retired from the Warden Service in 1936, but rather than relaxing at home in Banff, he spent his time looking after his wife, who had taken sick. Bill Peyto died of cancer in Banff on March 24, 1943, and was buried in the Old Banff Cemetery next to his beloved Emily.

On August 17, 1897, Peyto led Collie and Baker along Hector's route up the Bow and down the Mistaya to the Saskatchewan, arriving on August 23. They continued up the Saskatchewan then turned south along Howse River to do some climbing and exploring in the vicinity of the Freshfield Glacier. Poor weather and the threatened onset of winter pushed the party toward Howse Pass on September 3. Despite being fully versed in the history of the pass from Thompson to Wilson – and all of the difficulties involved – Collie chose it as his return route.

As he might have expected, Collie noted a marked change in the landscape on the western side of the Divide:

> The moment the Howse Pass is crossed a difference in the woods is at once noticed. They are much denser, and the difficulty of forcing a passage for the horses becomes greater. The Blaeberry Creek, down which our route lay, did not belie its reputation for being almost impassable for horses.... Our horses all day long were scrambling over huge trunks of fallen trees too thick to cut through, or climbing up and down the steep banks of the stream.[29]

A mere ten years after Moberly's trail had been cut, the route was again almost impassable. Proceeding downstream, travelling became even worse: "Next day we pushed down the valley, and the difficulty of getting the horses backwards and forwards over the stream and the fallen timber did not decrease, for the stream of course increased in volume every mile down the narrow valley."[30]

A little farther down the valley they came to an old trapper's cabin, obviously built for a single occupant, and wondered who would be willing to spend the winter in such a desolate place for the sake of a few marten skins. Just beyond the cabin, they found an opening with feed for the horses, and set up camp there. This was close to the spot Wilson had warned them the going would be hardest, so Peyto went on alone to investigate. He returned in the evening to report that the passageway was effectively blocked by fallen pine trees. Nature had again reclaimed its own.

In the meantime, the mountaineers had climbed a peak on the west side of the valley. As Collie later explained:

> From this point we were able to see a depression in the chain on the opposite side, which we thought might possibly lead to the north branch of the Kicking Horse River [Amiskwi], and so to Field on the Canadian Pacific Railway. In it lay our last hope, for to go back the way we had come would have taken about ten days, and our provisions were already nearly done.[31]

The depression Collie observed was in fact today's Amiskwi Pass, traditionally used by the Kootenay people en route to the Kootenay Plains. However, it is unlikely that the Kootenays used this route after the 1811 Peigan blockade of Howse Pass. They were probably driven from the mountains in the 1813–18 period,[32] and any traces of their route over Amiskwi Pass would have disappeared by 1897.

Although "this gap in the mountains to the south was below the tree limit, [Collie and his friends] recognised that great difficulty would probably be experienced in finding a trail up which horses could be taken."[33] Nevertheless, given the limited options before them, the men decided to seek out the pass. Beginning early the next day, they found that the initial climb was excessively steep. Fortunately, once they reached the top of the ridge, they were able to easily attain the pass. In spite of heavy snowfall overnight, they were able to cross the pass in brilliant sunshine on September 7. Two days later they arrived safely in Field.

Having determined that the Blaeberry River section of the Howse Pass trail was simply too difficult to serve as a passageway between the Saskatchewan and Columbia rivers, the members of Collie and Baker's party became the first non-Aboriginal people to cross what Collie named Baker Pass (Amiskwi Pass).[34] The route they had established became a popular alternative to the Bow Valley and Pipestone Pass[35] trails as a return route for pack trains in the Saskatchewan River area.

The Amiskwi valley in 2003, showing the results of a forest fire and logged-over areas in the background.

ADVENTURERS

The year after Peyto's initial trip across Baker Pass, he and packer/cook Roy Douglas led mountaineer Walter Wilcox on a late fall trip to the Saskatchewan River area.[36] They left on October 12 and travelled up the Bow to the Saskatchewan in miserable winter weather. The weather improved when they turned west toward Wilcox's main objective: Glacier Lake.

On October 20 they proceeded toward Howse Pass and the Blaeberry. Winter conditions made travelling difficult for their nine horses, and the situation deteriorated as they turned toward Amiskwi Pass. The horses were now weak from lack of feed; the eighteen inches (forty-six centimetres) of snow on the ground did nothing to expedite the journey. Guided by compass, it took another three days to reach Field, a distance of approximately thirty-three miles (fifty-three kilometres).

In 1900 mountaineer James Outram commented that the north side of Amiskwi Pass:

> has not found favour as a regular way, and if it be used as a means of communication between the Kicking Horse and upper waters of the Blaeberry or North Saskatchewan (now that fallen timber has rendered the lower Blaeberry valley impassable), it should be used on the southward journey alone, the danger of descending with horses on the farther side being considerable.[37]

Outram himself had not used the route, so his comments must have been based on discussions with others.

The following year, Outram did travel up the Amiskwi valley in the company of world-famous mountaineer Edward Whymper. The party consisted of the two mountaineers; two Swiss guides, Christian Klucker and Christian Häsler; and guide Tom Martin, supplied by Tom Wilson. They went as far as the mouth of Kiwetinok River, a tributary of the Amiskwi that arises near the pass of the same name and divides the valley of the Amiskwi River from that of the Little Yoho. Outram and Whymper went no farther, returning to Field the same day.[38]

Later that year, Tom Wilson joined Whymper's party (see Route II on page 106) in the Little Yoho Valley and guided Whymper and Klucker over the previously untried Kiwetinok Pass and down into the Amiskwi valley. They spent two very frustrating days struggling through unexplored territory before reaching Field. There are no other reports of anyone using this route from the top of Kiwetinok Pass; there is no trail there today.

In spite of James Outram's comments about travelling north over Amiskwi Pass with horses, an increasingly adventurous Mary Schäffer decided to do just that in 1906. This Pennsylvanian widow had overcome her fear of horses and camping in order to complete a guide to Rocky Mountain flora begun with her late husband, Charles. The project essentially complete, Schäffer was beginning to travel for the sheer pleasure of it. Her writings do not indicate what motivated her to attempt an ill-reputed pass; it may be that hearing someone advise against it was just the goad this plucky woman needed.

Tom Wilson supplied the outfit as he had done for Schäffer's previous travels, complete with a young Billy Warren to lead the group. They left Field on June 8, following the Amiskwi River to the pass, along the ridge, and down the steep trail to the Blaeberry River. Contrary to Outram's warning, they do not appear to have encountered any difficulties on the steep descent. From the Blaeberry, they followed Thompson's route over Howse Pass. They added a side trip to Glacier Lake, from whence they followed the well-worn route down the Howse and Saskatchewan rivers to the Kootenay Plains.[39] The following year, at the end of Schäffer's first summer-long expedition through the Rockies, Billy Warren guided the party home from the Kootenay Plains along this same route.

Once Schäffer's 1906 trip had established the feasibility of travelling north over Amiskwi Pass with horses, several others followed. In 1910 mountaineer J.E.C. Eaton[40] took his Italian cousin on a circular tour through the mountains. They left Field on July 15, accompanied by Swiss guide Heinrich Burgener, guide and packer Bruce Otto, and cook Glen Jordan. The five men and ten horses travelled a short distance north along Emerald Creek, turned west, crossed the creek and proceeded to reach the top of Baker (Amiskwi) Pass on July 17. They set up camp two hundred yards (183 metres) below the pass on the north side, close to where the parking lot is today.

By July 19 they had descended to the Blaeberry and crossed Howse Pass. They spent the night at the top of the pass before proceeding down to the gravel flats of the Howse River, where they set up a more permanent camp – just as David Thompson had over one hundred years earlier. They climbed and explored until August 1 then moved camp a short distance to Glacier Lake. They decided not to linger at the lake but to continue on their way home, arriving in Laggan on August 5.

Another mountaineer made his way north in 1920, intent on climbing in the Mount Forbes region southwest of Glacier Lake. Canada's own J.W.A. Hickson[41] and a young friend, E.L. Redford, set out for Howse Pass with Bert McCorkell and the two Legace brothers as guides, packers, and cooks. The Brewster outfitters at Lake Louise had fitted them up with fourteen horses and a month's worth of supplies.[42]

Instead of taking the leisurely route from Laggan over Bow Summit, the party decided to follow the Emerald River from Field. Missing the turnoff for the Amiskwi River, McCorkell ended up at Emerald Lake. Fortunately, he was able to take an upper trail west from the lake to the Kiwetinok River and then follow the usual trail north over Amiskwi Pass. After camping near the summits of both Amiskwi and Howse passes, they proceeded to set up camp on Forbes Creek, from which they climbed Mount Forbes. Further climbing on the Columbia Icefield rounded out the trip; they returned to Banff along the Bow Valley route.

Opposte above: J. Monroe Thorington (centre) in camp with Swiss guide Edward Feuz, Jr. (l) and mountaineer Howard Palmer.

Opposite below: Famous mountain guide Jimmy Simpson leading a pack train. Simpson is perhaps best known for building Num Ti Jah Lodge on the shores of Bow Lake.

Mountaineers' use of the trail continued on July 6, 1922, when a pack train of seventeen horses left Field to follow a trail up the Amiskwi River. J. Monroe Thorington, the leader of the group, declared it was a good trail that required no cutting – an abnormality in the mountains. Though he saw no need to repeat Outram's overzealous warning, he did feel obliged to comment that "the descent from Amiskwi Pass to the Blaeberry is over one of the steepest trails in the mountains."[43]

On July 10 Thorington's party, which consisted of fellow mountaineer Howard Palmer, Swiss guide Edward Feuz Jr., and guide Jimmy Simpson, set up their main camp on the Howse River west of Howse Pass, near the Freshfield Glacier. They remained until July 21,[44] then headed down the Howse River and returned home over Bow Summit, arriving in Lake Louise on July 25.

Scientists

After Peyto, Collie, and Baker re-established the trail, tourists travelling, climbing, and exploring the mountain wilderness constituted the bulk of the traffic over the old Kootenay route. But early in the summer of 1917, Howse Pass saw a group approach with a more utilitarian purpose. R.W. Cautley, A.O. Wheeler, and their crews had arrived with their surveying equipment.[45] All along the Continental Divide, members of the Boundary Commission were visiting the passes. Often, they followed the Divide between passes, occupying camera stations, and erecting monuments to mark the watershed. That summer, they were working south from Howse Pass to Bow Summit. Cautley and Wheeler spent a month surveying around Howse Pass.

Several years later, A.O. Wheeler, the influential president of the Alpine Club of Canada, suggested that a pack train retrace the Inter-provincial Boundary Survey parties' route between Field and Mount Robson. The first part of the trip would be along the now familiar Amiskwi Pass/Howse Pass route to the North Saskatchewan River.

In 1923 the Appalachian Mountaineering Club took up the pack train challenge.[46] A party of seventeen assembled near Field on July 15. They had no problems until they reached the Blaeberry River. It was in flood, as was Conway Creek, which leads from the top of Howse Pass down to the gravel flats of the Howse River. Much equipment was lost crossing these streams. Fortunately, they encountered no further problems; the party easily made its way to the Saskatchewan and on up the Alexandra River (see Route III on pages 153–172).

The only other scientific investigation in the Howse/Amiskwi Pass region took place late in the summer of 1919. Dr. Charles Walcott, the man who alerted the scientific community to the rich Burgess Shale beds (see Route II on pages 118–126), and his wife, Mary Vaux Walcott, spent most of a month studying the geology and collecting fossils around Glacier Lake, the Lyell Glacier, and Glacier Lake canyon.[47]

ESCORTED OUTFITTED TRIPS

In 1917 Caroline Hinman's first Off the Beaten Track trip had brought the popular phenomenon of escorted backcountry trips to the Canadian Rockies.[48] From then on, she travelled widely throughout the range, following nearly every existing trail and cutting some of her own. The groups she escorted tended to be large, with teenaged girls making up the bulk of her paying customers.

In the summer of 1924, she hired Jim Boyce and five assistants to guide her group of seventeen men, women, and teenaged girls along the old Kootenay Trail to the Saskatchewan River. They set out near Field, at the Natural Bridge on the Kicking Horse River. Lillian Gest, a lifelong friend of Caroline Hinman who often joined these trips, explained:

> When we left the Natural Bridge and started up the Amiskwi Trail we were leaving civilization behind and embarking on an adventure and a kind of life that was new to a good many of us. For some weeks we did not expect to reach any town or settlement of any kind. If we met anyone it would be only a forest or fire warden or perhaps a party like ourselves on a similar expedition. Once or twice we met a party of Indians spending the summer on their old hunting grounds along the Saskatchewan River.[49]

They travelled about fifteen miles (twenty-four kilometres) a day, setting off single file with Boyce in the lead, followed by Hinman and the paying guests. Recounted Gest: "As soon as breakfast was over, each of us put up his or her own lunch. Sandwiches were made from bannock which was baked fresh each night by the cook.... After breakfast and when lunch was made, we had our sleeping bags to roll up, duffle bags to close and have ready for the men to put them on the pack-horses."[50] After the guests departed, Boyce's men would finish breaking camp and then led the rest of the pack train onto the trail.

The Natural Bridge on the Kicking Horse River
as it appeared early in the twentieth century.

Two or three hours after setting out, the main party would break for lunch, then resume travelling another two to three hours until reaching a suitable campsite. "The first necessity of course was water," Gest explained. "The next pre-requisite was horse feed.... A level spot for the tents and a view were generally high on the list too.... When I think now of all the work that went into making and breaking camp every day I am appalled. No wonder we were glad to get into an old camp site and to find a nice supply of tent poles cut and stacked up against a tree."[51]

The 1924 party made their first camp on the Amiskwi River. The following night (July 11), they camped on the pass. The night of July 12 was spent along the Blaeberry River; the next day they moved to the top of historic Howse Pass, where they stayed for three days.

Every few days, Hinman liked to take a break at an attractive spot. That year, they paused another two days near the Freshfield Glacier, then camped by the main stream of the Saskatchewan River on the night of July 19. Another party, consisting of three mountaineers, two Swiss guides, and three wranglers had set up camp nearby. All thirty-two adventurers ate together that night before resuming their respective journeys. The Hinman party continued up the Alexandra River (See Route III on page 166), eventually arriving back in Banff on August 22 after approximately six weeks on the trail.

Four years later, Caroline Hinman – again accompanied by Lillian Gest – used the Howse Pass/Amiskwi Pass route to return home from a long trip to the north. The group was of similar size to her 1924 party. They started up the Howse River on August 19, descending the Amiskwi River on August 25. They spent their final night in the luxury of the Emerald Lake cabins before heading for Banff and home.

The Future

The trail over Howse Pass and down the Blaeberry River was first suggested as a route for the Canadian Pacific Railway in 1871. In 1906 the Bella Coola & Fraser Lake Railway proposed to build a line from Red Deer to the Pacific at Bella Coola over Howse Pass and down the Blaeberry. Neither proposal came to fruition. In the latter part of the twentieth century, the city of Red Deer repeatedly proposed a road through the Howse valley to connect the central Alberta city to the Trans-Canada Highway at Golden, providing a much shorter route to the coast. Although the Banff National Park Management Plan of 1988 precludes the construction of new roads in the park, there are renewed political pressures for construction of this road. Increasing traffic on the Trans-Canada through Banff is taken by some as sufficient justification for the proposed road over Howse Pass. We can only hope that the management plan of 1988 will be honoured, leaving the top of Howse Pass the beautiful wilderness it was when David Thompson camped there in 1807 with his wife and three children.

The author's campsite on Glacier Lake. The surroundings (other than the picnic table) would have looked much the same for the Hinman/Gest party and others that visited the lake early in the twentieth century.

The Trail Today

The Kootenay Plains mark the beginning of the historic Howse Pass trail. The trail along the south side of the North Saskatchewan River from the Siffleur River parking area to Highway 93 will mainly appeal to cyclists and day hikers who want a pleasant day trip from the Siffleur River area. Few, if any, will want to attempt the unmaintained section from the National Park boundary to Warden Lake. The continuation of the trail on the south side of the North Saskatchewan River – the route likely followed by David Thompson – requires a major ford of the Mistaya River. The best option for hikers is to go south three kilometres to a connector trail's bridge across the Mistaya.

Taking the Howse Pass/Amiskwi Pass route west of the Icefields Parkway (Highway 93) is a much larger commitment. The only alternative to following the entire 101-kilometre trail to Field is to exit along the forestry road down the Blaeberry River. (You would follow this road approximately sixty-three kilometres from the Ensign Creek junction to Golden.) Most hikers will require a minimum of five days to complete the route, but seven to eight days would be more relaxing.

There are no particular difficulties along the trail. The river fords are relatively easy. Only short sections require route-finding skills, and minimal ones at that. Though the only designated camping spot on the entire route is the BC forestry site at Cairnes Creek, there should be little problem finding suitable camping sites along the way – except perhaps along the forestry road leading up to the Ensign Creek valley. The route will mainly appeal to those who yearn for a peaceful backcountry experience where they will meet few if any other hikers.

The trail from the Siffleur River parking area through the broad valley of the North Saskatchewan River is often open with outstanding views. As far as the National Park boundary, the trail is very pleasant for hiking or cycling, with remnants of traplines along the route. I was fortunate enough to chat with a couple who currently run a trapline in the area. They were near an old mill site, working on their winter cabin. In summer they cross the river by boat, but in the winter they can cross on the ice. Most of their supplies are brought in during the winter.

Unfortunately the three kilometres between the park boundary and the Warden Lake trail (see trail guide on page 69) is not maintained. Fallen trees make passage very difficult. I did manage to get through with a bicycle but was often forced to carry the bike while scrambling over criss-crossed logs. Most cyclists will prefer to turn back at the park boundary. Bicycling is not permitted on the Warden Lake trail.

West of the Icefields Parkway, the trail from Mistaya Canyon to the top of Howse Pass is a gentle climb. The Howse River gravel flats where Thompson spent two weeks waiting for the snow to melt are a worthwhile destination in themselves. These open flats offer magnificent

A modern trap along the North Saskatchewan River
trail, part of a trapline that is run every winter.

views of the surrounding mountains and easy access to Glacier Lake – provided one has the means to cross the Howse River. This is a difficult or impossible ford for most hikers.

Fortunately, the modern-day hiking trail to Glacier Lake avoids the Howse River ford. Beginning on a trail just north of The Crossing tourist centre (junction of Highway 93 and the North Saskatchewan River), this trail with its bridge over the North Saskatchewan River makes for a relatively easy day hike or backpacking trip to an incredibly scenic lake. It does not, however, connect with the main Howse Pass trail.

The trail between the gravel flats and the top of the pass stays largely in the trees and is rather uninteresting, with no views of the surrounding mountains. The views from the top of the pass are pleasant but not spectacular, though the section from the top of the pass to the Cairnes Creek Recreation Site and the beginning of the forestry road is quite scenic.

The trail from the Kootenay Plains along the south side of the North Saskatchewan and Howse rivers, over Howse Pass, and down the Blaeberry River to the beginning of the forestry road is essentially the route followed by Thompson, Hector, Wilson, Peyto, and many others. When I arrived at the Cairnes Creek parking area, I found several men milling about a pickup truck and large horse trailer. Upon inquiry, I learned that the men had hauled some of the horses all the way from California to do some trail riding in a true wilderness area. One of the men was an aficionado of David Thompson history, eager to sleep at the top of Howse Pass where Thompson had spent the night nearly two hundred years earlier.

The continuation of the original fur-trade route down the Blaeberry to the Columbia, which presented such difficulties to early travellers, is now a forestry road. Little if any trace of the original pack trail remains. The hike down this remote forestry road can be long and boring unless one is lucky enough to be able to hitch a ride or has arranged for transportation ahead of time. Even from the comfort of a truck, one need only look off the road into the forest to gain an appreciation of what early travellers experienced on their forays into this wild country. I was fortunate enough to have my choice of rides. I initially arranged with the American trail riders to give me a lift down the Blaeberry River as far as the bridge. But before they were ready to go, the owner of the lodge in the Wildcat valley just east of the parking area appeared on the scene. The riders suggested I might prefer to go with him, as their heavy load would be slow on what is sometimes a very rough road.

Above: The forest along the Blaeberry River today, showing how difficult it would have been to make a trail.

Left: Historic marker on the Glacier Lake trail made by M.P. Bridgland's survey crew in 1928.

Near the point where Peyto turned east from the Blaeberry to climb the ridge, a branch forestry road crosses the river, takes numerous switchbacks through a clear-cut, and follows along the top of the ridge to a large parking lot near the base of Amiskwi Pass. Despite all its switchbacks, this road is still very steep, and I was unfortunate enough to have to walk most of the uphill portion on a very hot day. The parking area at the end of the road is quite unique: it is fenced to keep out porcupines, which chew on such essential automobile parts as brake lines, especially if these parts have a coating of salt from winter driving. When a vehicle arrives, its occupants have to open the enclosure, park inside, remove all items they are taking with them, and then reseal the fence as well as possible. The whole enclosure is somewhat makeshift, and it requires a bit of effort to succeed in foiling the animals.

The remainder of the route along the Amiskwi to the Kicking Horse River mainly follows old logging roads and an old fire road. The Amiskwi valley was logged until 1968 and clear-cuts are still visible, though the land is recovering. The roads, which are largely grown over with grasses and shrubs, make for pleasant hiking. I did not see anyone from the top of the pass to the Kicking Horse valley; the route has its charms for those who appreciate a quiet wilderness experience.

Trail Guide

Distances are adapted from existing trail guides: Patton and Robinson, Potter, and Beers, and from Gem-Trek maps. Distances intermediate from those given in the sources are estimated from topographical maps and from hiking times. All distances are in kilometres.

From the Kootenay Plains to Saskatchewan Crossing
(Hwy. 93)

Maps   82 N/15 Mistaya Lake
            82 N/16 Siffleur River
            83 C/1 Whiterabbit Creek
            83 C/2 Cline River
            Bow Lake and Saskatchewan Crossing (Gem Trek)

There is virtually no elevation change on this hike.

Trailhead

The east end of the trail begins at the Siffleur Falls parking lot and recreation area on Highway 11, 27 km east of Saskatchewan Crossing on Highway 93. The parking lot is in the Kootenay Plains Ecological Reserve and is clearly marked from the highway. The west end of the trail is 2 km south of the junction of Highways 93 and 11, 100 m south of the warden cabin.

0.0   Siffleur Falls parking lot.

0.7   From the parking lot, follow the wide track to the blue suspension bridge across the North Saskatchewan River and continue straight ahead on the boardwalk.

1.2   At the end of the boardwalk, turn sharply right (south) where there is a sign indicating a hiking trail. Continue ahead on an old bulldozed road.

6.0   Cross a small creek on a bridge; continue on the old road through a forest to the river's edge.

7.6   Sign indicates the end of the ecological reserve. The trail now passes through a trapping area. The blue plastic boxes along the way are part of a trapline.

10.4   Lookout structure beside the trail, probably part of the trapline.

12.0   Major bridge across Spreading Creek and the Wilderness Area boundary. There is a picnic table at this site. Although forested, there are still good views of the mountains on either side of the valley.

14.9   An open area with a bridge across a small creek and an old sawmill site. There is a new cabin off to the left (west), part of a winter trapline.

16.7   Major bridge across Corona Creek. Just beyond the bridge are a picnic table and a sign indicating that the area is maintained by the Rodpka family, undoubtedly volunteers who regularly use the area.

17.8   The trail swings left (south) to get around a high ridge and passes through a burned-out area. The road then curves back to the right (west), with the road forming the boundary between burned and unburned forest. It continues into a logged-out area.

25.2   Trail reaches the top of a ridge overlooking the river and continues steeply downhill to the edge of the river.

25.6   National Park boundary sign, warning that the trail is not maintained beyond this point. The trail continues as an old road made by some type of wheeled vehicle. It is not bulldozed. This rough trail follows fairly close to the river. It includes many hills, and is often criss-crossed by a maze of trees, making for very difficult passage, especially for those who choose to bicycle this trail. I saw no indication that anyone uses this portion of the trail.

27.5   Trail descends to the gravel flats by the river and reaches a major creek, over which a log has fallen, creating a natural bridge. After the creek, the trail becomes a narrow single track.

28.0   Ford a major creek that is wide but not deep. Continue along on the gravel flats of the river, then head back into the woods, where there is a good trail but a lot of deadfall.

29.0   Join a well-maintained trail. At a junction, the trail to Warden Lake goes to the left (south); continue straight ahead for Saskatchewan Crossing.

31.5   Trail ends at Highway 93 after passing the warden station corrals, visible in the background. The trailhead is just south of the warden cabin.

From Saskatchewan Crossing (Hwy. 93) to the Kicking Horse River

Maps   82 N/15 Mistaya Lake
        82 N/7 Golden
        82 N/10 Blaeberry River
        Bow Lake and Saskatchewan Crossing (Gem Trek)
        Lake Louise and Yoho (Gem Trek)

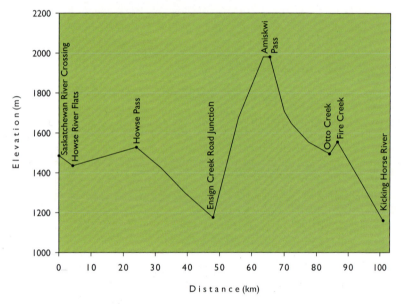

Trailhead

The trail can be attempted as a continuation of the above trail along the North Saskatchewan River, which is the route taken by David Thompson. However, this horse trail requires a major ford of the Mistaya River and is not recommended for hikers. A connector trail that uses the Mistaya Canyon bridge begins at the Mistaya Canyon parking area, 3 km south of the Saskatchewan Crossing Warden Station on the west side of Highway 93.

　　To begin at the south end of the trail, follow the Emerald Lake Road (2 km west of Field) to the Natural Bridge parking area, 1.5 km northwest of the Trans-Canada Highway. The gravel Kicking Horse Fire Road leads west from the parking area. In 1.9 km it reaches a picnic area and bridge across the Amiskwi River. The trail leads to the right (north) on the Amiskwi Fire Road after crossing the bridge.

0.0   Parking area for Mistaya Canyon. From the north end of the parking lot, proceed across the bridge, turn right (west), and climb up a steep bank.

3.1   Trail marker pointing toward Howse Pass. Continue on a good trail through the trees.

4.3   The horse trail from the warden cabin comes in from the right. There is another Parks sign here pointing to the Howse River, which is visible through the trees. The trail soon emerges on the Howse River flats and continues along on a bank on the southwest side of the river. The terrain is generally very open with great views of the surrounding mountains, Mount Outram in the west, Mount Sarbach and Kaufmann Peaks to the east.

9.0   Trail sign pointing to the right (northwest), to Glacier Lake. Following this trail requires a ford of the Howse River and is intended as a horse trail. It is not recommended for hikers. (See the trail guide to Glacier Lake on pages 76–77 for directions to the lake by foot.) Follow the trail that continues along the bank of the river and into the forest.

15.5   Trail emerges onto the river flats for a short while, then re-enters the forest and begins a gentle uphill climb, with occasional views of the river and mountains through the trees.

24.0   Trail junction. The trail to the right (west) leads to a warden cabin. An old painted sign points ahead: "Howse Pass, 2 miles [3.2 km]." Ford the creek or cross on an old log. The trail continues over old corduroy logs with bridges over wet spots, indicating that at one time the trail was heavily used and well maintained. The trail levels out before reaching the top of the pass, offering several good camping spots.

26.5   Stream crossing, can be crossed on rocks.

26.8   Top of Howse Pass, Historic Sites & Monuments board and plaque (see photo on page 31). Beyond the pass, there is a broad, lightly forested meadow with good views of the surrounding mountains.

28.7   Near the end of the meadow, there are two small ponds. The Blaeberry River is on the left (east); a well-beaten horse trail is in the forest to the right of the river. It drops sharply into a narrow valley.

31.7   Aluminum bridge over Lambe Creek, which comes pouring down over a series of waterfalls in a narrow mountainside ravine. There is an old outfitter's camp here with a good campground. The trail continues along the river for the most part, with good views to the east and southeast.

34.5   Cross a small stream. The terrain to the east becomes very open with good views.

37.1   Come to an old rock slide. The trail crosses along the bottom of the slide.

39.2   Cairnes Creek. Just before reaching the creek, there is a sign that reads "David Thompson Heritage Trail, Ministry of Forestry, Province of BC." At the creek, follow the trail upstream to a single log bridge. Cross the bridge and then return downstream to an off-highway vehicle trail. This trail eventually merges with an old logging road heading south.

39.9   Junction with a modern gravel road. The Blaeberry River forestry road continues ahead, directly south. To the east are a parking/camping area and a trail leading into the Wildcat valley. The next 24.5 km of the route are along BC forestry roads, suitable for vehicle use (preferably with high clearance). The Gem Trek map is superior for this part of the trip, as the topo map is somewhat confusing regarding the location of the logging roads. Once you are in the Ensign Creek valley, the topo map can be used. Continue south on the gravel road that follows close to the

Blaeberry River on its west side. Almost all traces of the old horse trail were lost when the road was constructed.

48.0   Road junction. The Blaeberry River road continues to the southwest and eventually connects with the Trans-Canada Highway north of Golden.[52] To reach Amiskwi Pass, turn right (east) on the Ensign Creek logging road and cross the river on a road bridge. The junction of the two roads is clearly marked. The Ensign Creek road follows a northeast direction and begins a series of switchbacks as it climbs a steep ridge. As the elevation increases, the views down the valley continue to improve. Near the top of the switchbacks, a sign in a tree reads "Amiskwi Pass trail." In July 2003, a few metres of the trail had been cleared, but otherwise the trail appeared to be unused and difficult to follow. This may be part of the original horse trail between Howse and Amiskwi passes. Continue uphill on the logging road.

55.8   Road junction. The road to the left (northeast) goes up the Collie Creek valley. Keep to the right along the Ensign Creek valley. The road continues fairly straight to the south, ending near Amiskwi Pass.

63.5   The road ends at a parking lot. A well-used trail leads straight ahead, and in a short distance there is a substantial sign in a tree pointing left to Amiskwi Lodge and right to Amiskwi Pass. By continuing in the general direction of the sign and staying to the right of the slope, it is relatively easy to bushwhack to the Amiskwi meadows and the National Park boundary, where a clear trail begins. This is the route most hiking books recommend. However, you can travel the whole route on a trail, though it is a slightly longer route. Turn to the right (west) at the south end of the parking lot and follow a faint trail west down a gully toward Ensign Creek. Just before the creek, turn sharply to the left (south). Proceed south across a gravel bed and follow a good trail along the bank above the creek.

65.5   Signs mark the boundary of Yoho National Park at the north end of a small meadow. The trail continues along the left (east) side of the meadow. Soon after the meadow, the trail splits, with the right branch leading to a warden cabin. Continue to the left (south) through a small meadow, followed by open forest. This is a very picturesque area.

67.7   Enter a completely burned-out area, where many burned trees were still standing in 2003. The area had been logged prior to the fire and the trail follows an old logging road down the Amiskwi River. Amiskwi Falls is visible in the distance.

69.9   Ford the Amiskwi River just before the outflow from Amiskwi Falls. This is an easy ford. There is an old Parks bridge across the river, built in 1987 and now in poor shape. From here, the trail follows the west side of the river. (This route appears to be at odds with other guides. The old bridge clearly shows that the trail crosses the river. However, other guides appear to indicate that the trail continues as a single track on the east side of the river, after crossing the outflow from Amiskwi Falls. This route may still be possible but I did not see a trail. The two routes recombine in 4 km.) The trail along the west side of the river is faint in places but easy to follow. Just beyond a big knob of a hill on the right, you arrive at a flat, marshy area. The bits of timbers and building materials scattered about suggest an old logging mill site. This area is quite evident on the topo map.

72.1   Just beyond the marshy area, it is necessary to ford the Amiskwi River. Although the ford is not obvious, it should be easy for most to find. In 2003 there were piles of old logs on either side of the river. If in doubt, cross the river to the east side and follow it to the old Amiskwi Fire Road. Follow the road east, then south past a steel post with a Parks sign on the ground nearby. Continue following the old road along the side of the mountain, soaking in the good views down the valley.

75.7   The old road drops down to the river and crosses a creek on the remains of an old bridge. Continue along east of the river.

77.4   Ford the river (calf deep) to the west side and follow the old road northwest across the valley. Climb high on the west side before heading south, where there are again good views across the valley. The whole area was heavily logged some time ago.

80.7   Enter mature forest.

84.0   Otto Creek Bridge. Just beyond the bridge, the trail branches to the right (west) up Otto Creek to the Otto Creek Warden Cabin. Keep left. The trail climbs up out of the valley and high on the west side to Fire Creek.

86.5   Large open area, once a mill site. There is an old bridge upstream of the site and a newer bridge downstream. Cross the newer bridge and continue high on the west side of the valley, where there are long stretches of old road built up with timbers. There are good views to the north until the old road enters heavy forest.

98.2   The mountains on the south side of the Kicking Horse River come into view. The old road drops steadily into the Kicking Horse valley.

101.0 Trailhead and bridge across the Amiskwi River at the Kicking Horse River.

From Saskatchewan Crossing to Glacier Lake

Maps   82 N/15 Mistaya Lake
        Bow Lake and Saskatchewan Crossing (Gem Trek)

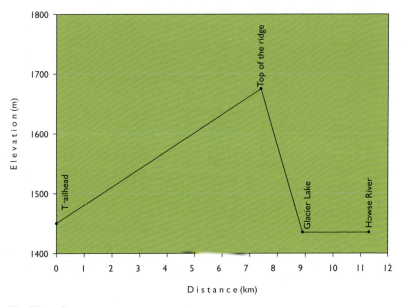

Trailhead

The trailhead parking lot is on the west side of Highway 93, 1 km northwest of the junction of Highways 11 and 93.

0.0   Trailhead parking lot. From here, a wide, well-made trail drops down through a young pine forest.

1.2   North Saskatchewan River bridge. River flows through a narrow gorge and continues through a young spruce/pine forest.

2.3   Spectacular viewpoint overlooking the meadows and gravel flats of the Howse River. The trail initially drops down to the river then leaves the river and heads into the woods.

4.5   Cross a stream on a log bridge, the first of four crossings in the next 1.5 km. After the final crossing, the trail begins to climb over a ridge through heavy forest.

7.4   Top of the ridge; start downhill in heavy forest. You soon get glimpses of the lake through the trees.

8.3   Painted sign in the trees, pointing toward the Saskatchewan River bridge. Just beyond the sign is a tree with a trail marker carved into it. The sign says "1928 Topographical Survey, M.P. Bridgland, DLS." There are ten names in total on the marker. A short distance farther, there are another painted sign and a modern sign. The trail branches here, with the trail to the lake continuing ahead and a horse trail going to the left (southeast) toward the Howse River.

The horse trail is likely similar to the route taken by David Thompson. A short distance along, there is a viewpoint overlooking the outflow from the lake. The well-travelled trail reaches a viewpoint above the gravel flats of the Howse River in 1.6 km, with a view toward Howse Pass. The trail stays on the bank above the Glacier Lake outflow for 2.4 km until a sign pointing to the lake. From here, horses ford the Howse River and join up with the Howse Pass trail. This ford is not recommended for hikers.

8.9   Shore of Glacier Lake. The campground is a short distance east along the lake. At the end of the campground is a small log cabin, still in good condition.

12.8   Near the west end of the lake. The trail mainly follows the shoreline along the lake but at times goes high above the lake to avoid steep banks. There are many old campsites along the lake, as well as gravel beds where streams have carried debris into the lake during periods of high runoff. At the end of the lake, the trail continues along a flat, meadow-like area on the gravel flats before gradually becoming indistinct.

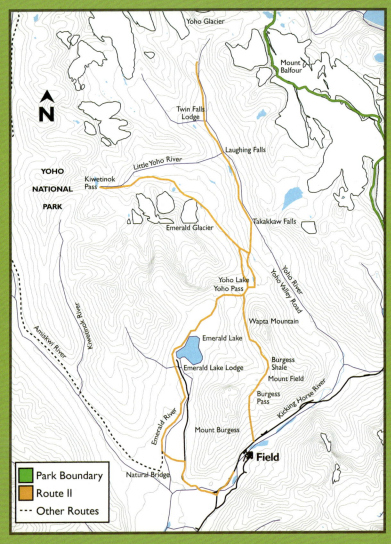

Route II from Field to the Yoho Glacier over Yoho Pass and from Field to Kiwetinok Pass over Burgess Pass.

Route II

Controversy amidst the Falls: Trails from the Kicking Horse River to the Yoho Valley

The campground at the west end of Little Yoho Valley is the most remote camping spot in the busy Yoho Valley area. While I was camping there with two male friends, one of us noticed that someone had left large chunks of moss in the privy. We hypothesized the backpacker's worst nightmare: someone had run out of toilet paper. The only other people in the campground were a young couple from the eastern United States. We had spoken with them earlier in the day and were somewhat surprised to find that despite being a long way from home in an unfamiliar mountainous environment, they were well equipped and seemed to be experienced in backpacking.

We did not see them again until morning. They were just leaving the cooking area as we arrived. After some chit-chat, one of my companions casually asked, "Hey, did you guys run out of toilet paper?" The reaction was priceless.

The young woman shyly glanced at her husband, turned her eyes back to the man who had asked the question, then back to her husband before eventually quietly responding, "Well, yes we did, but how did you know?" We described the moss in the privy. The woman immediately replied, "Oh, that wasn't us; we've been using coffee filters."

After we all had a good laugh, I slipped back to our tent, got my "spare" supply, and quietly handed it to the young woman. Her big smile and quiet "thank you" spoke volumes. Before leaving, the young couple wanted to take a picture of the three backpackers with bald heads and grey beards, as a memory of their trip and perhaps of the coffee filter incident. I still find it difficult to make my morning cup of coffee without smiling to myself.

Chronology

1882 Tom Wilson follows horse tracks into an adjacent valley while searching for his pack horses and discovers Emerald Lake.

1884 Tom Wilson and Jim Wright follow the Yoho River from the Kicking Horse River past Takakkaw Falls and Twin Falls to prospect in the Yoho Valley.

1887 J.J. McArthur climbs Burgess Pass, the first white man to do so.

1891 Samuel Allen follows Wilson's route along the Emerald River to the lake.

1892 William Brymner and John Hammond paint near Field, not straying far from the railway.

1897 Professor Jean Habel carries out the first real exploration of the Yoho Valley. From Field, he and his party travel to Emerald Lake and over Yoho Pass to Takakkaw Falls, then north along the Yoho River to the Yoho Glacier. They return by following Wilson's route down the Yoho River.

Tom Wilson and Jimmy Simpson lead fourteen members of the Philadelphia Photographic Society to Emerald Lake.

Simpson escorts Miss Brunstermann and Agnes Laut to Emerald Lake on trails being cut by the CPR.

1900 The CPR extends its trail from Emerald Lake over Yoho Pass to Takakkaw Falls.

1901 The CPR continues its trail from Takakkaw Falls to Twin Falls.

John Hammond makes use of the new trails to cross Yoho Pass and continue on to Takakkaw Falls and the Yoho Glacier.

Edward Whymper visits Emerald Lake and has his men finish cutting a trail to Yoho Pass, then west to the Little Yoho Valley.

Tom Wilson's stray horses led him to Emerald Lake, where the animals had likely been earlier with their Aboriginal owners.

At Whymper's suggestion, the CPR cuts a trail over Burgess Pass and along the slopes of Wapta Mountain to Yoho Pass, today's Wapta Highline trail.

1901   The Vaux family returns to Emerald Lake and proceeds to the Yoho Valley over Yoho Pass, although a large number of men were still working on the trail. Mary Vaux becomes the first woman recorded to see the valley.

1901   Mountaineer James Outram and his brother, William, walk to Emerald Lake at night. The next day, they proceed to Yoho Pass and return to Field by an alpine route.

1902   The CPR completes the fourteen-room Emerald Lake Chalet and builds a buggy road to service it.

1904   Mrs. Mary de la Beach-Nichol hires guide Jimmy Simpson to take her to Emerald Lake. She walks with botanist John Macoun as far as the lake. Macoun proceeds to the Yoho Glacier.

Mary Schäffer and companions hire Tom Wilson to take them on a trip to the Yoho Valley.

Elizabeth Parker travels by horseback as far as the viewpoint overlooking Takakkaw Falls before returning to Field via Burgess Pass.

Construction of a wagon road along the Yoho River to Takakkaw Falls begins.

1906   The Alpine Club of Canada holds its first annual camps at Yoho Lake.

1909   The road to Takakkaw Falls is completed.

1909   Late in the summer, Dr. Charles Walcott and his family ride the newly completed road to Takakkaw Falls and move on to the Burgess Pass area. On August 31, they discover what proves to be the single most important fossil find in the world, the Burgess Shale.

1909   Canadian Pacific Railway publicist John Murray Gibbon takes his first outfitted trip in the Rockies, a figure-eight loop around the Emerald Lake/Yoho Valley region.

1911   Federal Forest Rangers begin regular patrols in the Emerald Lake/Yoho Valley region.

1916   The Warden Service clears all of the trails in the Emerald Lake/Yoho Valley region of deadfall.

Portrait artist J.S. Sargent spends part of the summer in the Yoho Valley, mainly around Twin Falls.

1917   Walcott reports that after working the Burgess Shale quarry (today's Walcott Quarry) for up to six weeks each summer, the quarry is played out.

1923   John Murray Gibbon and friends inaugurate the Trail Riders of the Canadian Rockies. Their first ride starts in Field, with the first night's camp near Takakkaw Falls.

A plaque honouring Tom Wilson as "Trailblazer of the Canadian Rockies" is unveiled.

1924   The Walcotts travel to the Takakkaw Falls bungalow camp by car and spend only a short time at the quarry before returning to the Yoho Valley for a Trail Riders gathering. It is Walcott's last summer in the Yoho Valley.

Lawren Harris visits Emerald Lake, Takakkaw Falls, and the Waterfall Valley, painting in each location.

Caroline Hinman leads a large group up the Yoho Valley Road and on to Twin Falls. They complete a loop through the Little Yoho Valley and return to Emerald Lake along the Highline and Yoho Pass trails.

History

Pioneering the Routes

The Yoho Valley and Emerald Lake areas are unusual in that there is no evidence that fur traders or other early explorers and adventurers travelled into these regions. Early railway surveyors do not appear to have wandered into these remote valleys, either, despite the fact that they were working along the nearby Kicking Horse River.

Even Aboriginal peoples appear to have seldom visited these valleys. Perhaps this is because the area, which has been described as "a dangerous and forbidding maze of mountains that did not invite travel,"[1] was less than ideal animal habitat. Three campsites at the mouth of the Emerald River dating back to 1800 constitute the only archaeological finds in the area, and while the Kootenay and other mountain peoples likely used a trail along this river to hide from their enemies in remote mountain valleys, they appear to have been driven from the mountains in the 1813–18 period. There is no evidence that they – or any other Aboriginal peoples – travelled in the adjacent Yoho Valley.

It was well into the nineteenth century before the first recorded non-Aboriginal explorer made his way into the valley. In 1882 Tom Wilson had been hauling freight for the Canadian Pacific Railway (CPR) from Padmore (Kananaskis) to the end of the tote road along the Kicking Horse River. He had two strings of packhorses, one of which he would leave to feed and rest near the Natural Bridge west of Kicking Horse Pass while he put the other to work.

One day the horses went missing. Wilson tracked them past the Natural Bridge, where he noted they had begun walking in single file, as if they were following a leader to a familiar place. Following their hoofprints along the Emerald River, Wilson tracked them to a beautiful lake, known today as Emerald Lake. "For a few moments," he later explained, "I sat on

The view of the Yoho Valley that Tom Wilson
would have seen from near the top of Kicking
Horse Pass.

my horse and enjoyed the rare, peaceful beauty of the scene, then at the far end of the lake I noticed something move. It was an old white horse that belonged to my bunch and which we had bought from the Stoneys."[2] The lake had never before been seen by a white man, but Wilson surmised that the Native ponies had been there before and remembered the luscious meadows at the end of the lake.

An astute observer like Tom Wilson would have caught glimpses of the Yoho Valley each time he took his pack train across Kicking Horse Pass. So it is not surprising that two years after discovering Emerald Lake, he, his partner Jim Wright, and another man decided to go prospecting in Yoho Valley. They blazed a trail up the Yoho River to Takakkaw Falls then on to Laughing Falls and Twin Falls. They did not, however, name any of these features. Despite later controversy (see pages 91–92), this visit to Takakkaw Falls and the Yoho Valley was almost certainly the first by white men and perhaps by anyone.[3]

The next incursion into the area occurred in 1887. Between Wilson's trails up the Yoho and Emerald rivers lie two majestic mountains: Mount Field and Mount Burgess. The pass between them, known today as Burgess Pass, provides a third route to Emerald Lake and Takakkaw Falls. Surveyor J.J. McArthur is the first person known to have climbed the pass. He toiled doggedly without any sight of his destination until, "through those roadways cleared by the slide, we caught occasional glimpses of Mount Field, and struggled on with renewed vigor."[4] Trails connecting the pass to Yoho Lake (often referred to as Summit Lake) and Emerald Lake only came later.

The last major trail into the Yoho Valley was established as the result of pioneering work by Professor Jean Habel. His main interest, it seems, was to assess the possibility of climbing Mount Balfour, which had previously been attempted – unsuccessfully – from the east. Tom Wilson, now in the outfitting business, supplied Habel with guide Ralph Edwards, packer Fred Stephens, cook Frank Wellman, their horses, and four pack horses. Habel himself chose to walk, as mountaineers often did to condition themselves for a climb.

J.J. McArthur, the surveyor who first climbed Burgess Pass. A lake, a pass, and a creek in Yoho National Park are named after him.

Jean Habel (c.1845–1902)

Tall, dignified, and aristocratic-looking, Dr. Jean Habel was a German mathematics professor from Berlin. Little is known of his early life. As an adult, he became a member of the German–Austrian Alpine Club and gained high regard in the mountaineering community for his considerable climbing and exploration in the Alps and the Andes.

He first came to Canada in 1896; that year he travelled by rail for brief visits to Banff, Lake Louise, and Field. One particular mountain to the north of Field caught his attention as he passed through, and he returned to explore the following year. The account he published in the 1896–98 edition of *Appalachia* describing these explorations in the Yoho Valley generated considerable controversy over the years, especially with Tom Wilson (see page 42). While Wilson claimed to have been the first non-Aboriginal person to visit the region, the honour was attributed to Habel because he was the first to write about it.

Habel returned to the Rockies in 1901 to explore the region at the source of the Athabasca River and the Fortress Lake area. Though both Coleman and Wilcox had previously visited the lake, the area had been burned over, making it difficult to find. In spite of efforts to locate the trail blazes left by earlier explorers, progress was so slow that the party ran out of food and had to hurry back to civilization before completing its explorations. During that winter, Habel made extensive plans with Tom Wilson for a major trip the following summer, but on the eve of the professor's departure, Wilson received a wire announcing his sudden passing.

Professor Jean Habel, a loner who explored extensively in the Yoho Valley and near the headwaters of the Athabasca River.

On his two trips, Habel conducted valuable exploration in the Rockies and undoubtedly did a great deal to promote the Yoho Valley. However, like many men of his generation and upbringing, he was overbearing and dictatorial in his dealings with the men he hired to take him into the wilderness. He had particular difficulties with his cook, Fred Ballard. On hearing of the death of the professor, Ballard was heard to mutter, "Good, he can see the blazes now."[5]

The peak Habel first saw from the train, which he called "Hidden Mountain" because it kept appearing and disappearing from the train window, was named Mount Habel by fellow mountaineer J.N. Collie. However, post-First World War anti-German sentiment led to its name being changed to Mont des Poilus, in honour of French soldiers. In 1984 Graeme Pole, a mountain writer intimately involved with his subject, suggested that an unnamed peak on the Continental Divide, known for years as North Rhondda, be named Mount Habel in honour of the German professor. The name was officially accepted the following year. Habel Creek in Jasper National Park is also named after him.

Habel's 1897 party left Field on the morning of July 15, following a good trail past the Natural Bridge to Emerald Lake, where they stopped for lunch. Finding no defined trail beyond the lake, the men ferried their packs across on a raft and proceeded to drive the horses along the shore. Eventually, Habel reported, they came to an old trail, which they followed to Yoho Lake. This may have been a game trail, since there is no evidence of Aboriginal use, nor reports of earlier easterners having crossed Yoho Pass.[6]

Habel's party continued on past Yoho Lake, descending to Takakkaw Falls and the Yoho Valley. Habel was most impressed by what Edwards claims he always referred to as the "great fall."[7] "The torrent from the hanging glaciers, which cover the eastern terraces of the valley," Habel wrote, "... descended directly opposite to us in a very powerful waterfall. Rushing from under the ice at about the height of our standpoint, this fall plunges over a nearly perpendicular wall down to the very level of the valley bottom in beauty and grandeur hardly to be excelled by any other on our globe."[8]

After camping near the base of the "great fall," they proceeded on to Twin Falls and the spectacular Yoho Glacier. Edwards wrote:

> At first sight ... the most noticeable point about the glacier ... was the huge ice cave in which it terminated.... I found the cave to be of considerable size; as nearly as I could estimate I judged it to be about 25 feet [7.6 metres] high at its mouth and from 30 to 35 feet [9.1 to 10.6 metres] in width. The cave penetrated the ice mass for some 50 to 60 feet [15.2 to 18.3 metres], the roof sloping gently downwards and the sides gradually drawing inwards until at about the distance given, the cave came to an end.[9]

Unfortunately, this spectacular cave has long since disappeared due to glacial melt.

Habel's party spent most of three days exploring the glacier and adjacent mountain before returning along Wilson's route down the Yoho River to the Kicking Horse and on to Field. Habel was the only occupant of Mount Stephen House in Field when Collie, Baker, and Peyto arrived from their historic trip over Baker (Amiskwi) Pass (see Route I on pages 45–50).

This early period of exploration in the Yoho Valley has always been somewhat controversial. Throughout his life, Tom Wilson was adamant that he had been first to explore Yoho Valley. He wrote:

> With two others I went up the North Fork as we called it, past the Great Falls, past Laughing Falls and round by Twin Falls, in 1884. We were prospecting for minerals. In 1897 in order to get the CPR interested in this region, I got a German professor [Habel] to go in and take photos and write it up in the magazines. I gave him three men – Frank Wellman, Fred Stephens, and Ralph Edwards – and seven head of horses, provisions, tents etc. all for $7.00 per day and it cost me $11.50 per day cash and then the dam German took all the credit![10]

It is normal for the first person writing about an area to be credited with discovering it. However, Habel himself never claimed to have been the first in the Yoho Valley – his guide Ralph Edwards did.

In 1950 Edwards described the Yoho Valley as "a country … about which no one, from Wilson down, could give us the slightest information."[11] Edwards's writings make it clear that somewhere in the fifty years between the trip and the article, he and Wilson had had a falling out. Taken together, the quarrel, the time lapse, and Edwards's colourful and flowery writing style challenge the credibility of his comments.

Regardless, there is no record of anyone using Tom Wilson's route up the Yoho River to reach the Yoho Valley prior to the construction of the road to Takakkaw Falls in the early 1900s. Indeed, very few parties even visited Emerald Lake until the CPR began to cut such trails in hopes that its patrons' vacation experiences would be enhanced sufficiently to encourage them to return – with friends.

Opposite above: Tom Wilson's route up the Yoho Valley toward the Yoho Glacier would have passed through today's Laughing Falls Campground, where this mother goat and kid were spotted, far from their normal haunts on lofty mountain peaks.

Opposite below: The spectacular Yoho Glacier Cave, as Habel and his party would have seen it.

EMERALD LAKE

Nine years after Tom Wilson's horses led him to Emerald Lake, Samuel Allen, quickly gaining repute as one of the first mountaineers in the Lake Louise area, followed in his footsteps along the Emerald River.

The year was 1891, and Allen explained that the town of Field was

> a busy rendezvous for the prospectors, attracted by wild rumours of mineral wealth in the Ottertail range. One of these prospectors accompanied me next day on a trip to the lake by the way of the Natural Bridge. Crossing at this wild cañon the Kicking Horse, we ascended the heavy timber of a west spur of Mount Burgess until meeting the trail, which further east turned from the river bank. Throughout its entire length of some 10 miles [sixteen kilometres] it maintains nearly a constant level, crossing Emerald [River] and reaching the wooded bank of the lake, wherein lay mirrored the great rock peak upon whose ridge I had so lately stood…. This entire region, being still unharmed by fires, possesses a charm which is not even exceeded by the more snowy Selkirks.[12]

Another seven years passed before human feet again trod the shores of Emerald Lake.

In 1898, the year after Habel had journeyed past the lake and over Yoho Pass, fourteen members of the Philadelphia Photographic Society travelled across the continent in a private railway car[13] to visit Emerald Lake. The group, which included the Vaux and Schäffer families, asked Tom Wilson to outfit their expedition. Jimmy Simpson, then just starting out on his notable alpine career, was assigned to the party as cook.

Opposite above: (l–r) Unknown, Samuel Allen, C.S. Thompson, H.P. Nichols, and unknown. Allen walked along the Emerald River to become the second recorded non-Aboriginal person to see Emerald Lake.

Opposite below: Emerald Lake seen from Burgess Pass. Note the avalanche path on the north side of the lake and the alluvial fan on the east that is gradually filling the lake.

By the time Simpson escorted a Miss Brunstermann and Agnes Laut to the lake later that year, the CPR was already busy cutting trails. Laut, a Winnipeg schoolteacher, was a favourite of Norman Luxton, an adventurer, journalist, entrepreneur, and promoter who helped turn Banff into a premier tourist destination and later became known as "Mr. Banff." She can be credited with introducing Luxton to the works of Rudyard Kipling, whose adventure stories captured both of their imaginations and undoubtedly influenced Luxton later in life.[14]

Below: Emerald Lake Cabins, shortly after completion, circa 1906.

Opposite: This view of the town of Field and Mount Dennis would have provided a scenic backdrop for surveyor J.J. McArthur as he toiled upward on the first ascent of Burgess Pass.

Yoho Pass, Iceline, and Burgess Pass Trails

The fact that none of the early outfitters visited the Yoho Valley with their clients indicates that it held little interest for adventuresome travellers and mountaineers. A trip up the Yoho Valley could not easily be used as part of a route for a longer trip; it was essentially a dead-end valley surrounded by glaciers. The only possible exit route – over Kiwetinok Pass – was never developed.

Nevertheless, the CPR decided to exploit its potential interest to less adventurous tourists. In 1900 railway employees developed a trail along Habel's route past Emerald Lake to Yoho Pass and on to Takakkaw Falls. The following year the route was extended to Twin Falls. Once trails were cut, the valley was regularly visited by tourists – generally on short trips out of Field or Lake Louise – who were fortunate to have such spectacular scenery so close by. In 1902 the

CPR completed the fourteen-room Emerald Lake Chalet, its first log tourist lodge, and a buggy road to service it.[15]

But tourists were not the only people captivated by the scenic Yoho Valley. Recognizing the tremendous promotional value of well-crafted landscape paintings, the CPR offered selected artists free passes for transportation along its lines in return for paintings rendered. John Hammond, professor of fine arts at New Brunswick's Mount Allison University, was among those who took advantage of the offer.

JOHN HAMMOND (1843–1939)

John Hammond was an artist, teacher, world traveller, and mountain explorer. He was born in Montreal on April 11, 1843, and began working in his father's marble-cutting business at the age of nine. By the age of eleven, he had decided to become an artist, a vocation he followed for the rest of his long life.

In addition to his artistic skill, Hammond was endowed with a spirit of adventure and desire to travel. From 1860 to 1863 he apprenticed in the drapery business. In 1866 he took part in quelling a Fenian raid in Upper Canada. That same year, he left Canada for an extended trip to England and New Zealand, where he spent two and a half years panning for gold. He returned to Canada in 1869.

The following year, he accepted a position with Wm. Notman & Son, photographers, in Montreal. Through his work, he met photographer Benjamin Baltzy, to whom he volunteered to assist on an assignment to determine the best route for a transcontinental railway for the Geological Survey of Canada (GSC).

The GSC party made its way from Montreal across the United States to Victoria, then sailed up the Fraser River to Yale. From there the adventurers journeyed by stagecoach east to Kamloops, where the expedition – which consisted of 120 horses and mules, sixty packers, and six officers – was formed. The entire trip lasted from June to December. During this time, the party was successful in reaching Yellowhead Pass, although winter overtook them before they were able to return to Kamloops, causing great hardship.

Hammond continued travelling and painting, and in 1878 left Montreal for an extended sketching and painting tour of the eastern United States en route to an appointment with the Saint John, New Brunswick, branch of Wm. and J. Notman.

John Hammond, artist, teacher, world traveller, and mountain explorer, took advantage
of the CPR's offer of free transportation in
exchange for art.

He was promoted to branch manager in 1883, but left the following year to join the Owens Art Institution in Saint John. Alongside his work at the institution, he travelled and exhibited in Europe.

Hammond also formed a friendship with Sir William Van Horne, chairman of the Canadian Pacific Railway. In 1891 Van Horne commissioned him to paint the scenery along the CPR, resulting in trips to the Rockies in 1891–92 and again in 1901. His earlier trips were spent mainly painting along the railway, but in 1901 he headed into the backcountry for different mountain perspectives. That year he also travelled to the United States, Japan, and China, where he barely escaped with his life during a Boxer uprising.

In 1894 Hammond had left Saint John for Sackville, NB, to begin a university teaching career at Mount Allison University's new Owens Museum of Fine Arts. He continued to teach, paint, and exhibit until his retirement from teaching in 1919. He died in Sackville on August 10, 1939, at the age of ninety-six.

Having experienced the hardships entailed by early mountain travel on the 1871 GSC survey expedition, Hammond did not stray far from the railway when he returned to the Rockies in 1892 with fellow artist William Brymner.[16] When Hammond returned in 1901, he made Field his headquarters, reporting: "My trip this year was of more than usual interest from the fact that the country explored was entirely off the beaten track, part only being opened up to the most adventurous tourists and mountain climbers."[17]

It seems that the CPR's new trails were bolstering Hammond's sense of adventure. Hiring a packer and a Swiss guide, he spent a week at Emerald Lake – recently made accessible by the CPR's wagon road. They explored the mountains in the immediate vicinity of the lake, then took advantage of the new trail to move on to Yoho Pass and Yoho Lake. Deep snow prevented them from continuing any farther, so they returned to Field.

Hammond continued exploring and painting around Moraine Lake. Ten days later the snow had melted sufficiently for him and his assistants to spend a week camping at the look-off over Takakkaw Falls. They proceeded to descend to Yoho Valley near the base of Takakkaw Falls, then continued on to the Great Wapta Glacier (Yoho Glacier) and Twin Falls. Hammond declared: "The whole valley is perhaps the most magnificent piece of mountain scenery in the Canadian Rockies and trails are now being cut so that its wonders can be seen and enjoyed with comparative ease and comfort."[18]

In fact, Hammond was undoubtedly the first person to use this trail – and the first visitor to the Yoho Valley since Habel – although most books assign this credit to the Vaux family (see page 107).[19] Hammond made some thirty to forty sketches on this trip, some of which he later worked up into large paintings. The CPR continued its patronage over the next

decade, and Hammond became recognized as the railway's leading artist.

That same year, the CPR, always seeking publicity that would increase passenger flow to the mountains, had arranged for Edward Whymper to spend the summer around Lake Louise and Field. As the first person to climb the Matterhorn in the Alps, Whymper was undoubtedly the most famous mountaineer of his time.

Takakkaw Falls as Hammond would have seen them from the viewpoint on the Iceline Trail.

EDWARD WHYMPER (1840–1911)

Edward Whymper was born in London, England, on April 27, 1840, the son of an artist. It was his profession as a wood engraver that first led him to the mountains; a commission to do a series of alpine scenery sketches resulted in several trips to the Alps. Whymper ended up accomplishing many climbs in the Alps – especially the Mont Blanc group – between 1861 and 1865 and was able to provide much information on the topography of this poorly mapped area.

In 1865 he became the first mountaineer to climb the Matterhorn. The price of this distinction was enormous. Four of his companions died on the descent; Whymper himself was only saved by a broken rope. There was much speculation as to whether or not the rope had been cut, but the investigation did not find any evidence to support this theory. Whymper claimed to have been haunted for the rest of his life by the sight of his comrades falling to their deaths. Some speculate that it was this incident that led to his alcoholism later in life, although his brother, who did not witness such trauma, was also an alcoholic.

Whymper's first book, *Scrambles among the Alps* (1871), describes his attempts on the Matterhorn, including the unfortunate accident. He subsequently carried out explorations and climbs in Greenland and South America, publishing books on the Andes and on the use of the aneroid barometer at high altitudes.

In 1900 the Canadian Pacific Railway invited Whymper, the world's best-known mountaineer, to visit the Canadian Rockies. He returned several times, but alcoholism had already taken its toll and he was well past his prime as a mountaineer. His intention was to make a series of climbs and, in return for free transportation for himself and his four Swiss guides, promote the

Edward Whymper gained world fame as the first person to climb the Matterhorn. His work in the Canadian Rockies provided publicity for the CPR.

CPR in his writings and lectures. He came to the Rockies every summer from 1901 to 1905, then made one final visit in 1909.

The CPR management held great expectations for Whymper's sojourn in the Rockies, but little was accomplished. Today Canadians remember him mainly for his legendary drink-

ing, his inability to get along with virtually everyone he associ-
ated with, and the practical jokes played on him by the men in
his employ. He died two years after his final visit to the Rockies,
on September 16, 1911. He is buried in Chamonix, France.

Outfitter Tom Wilson, selected by the CPR to provide for Whymper's
needs, assigned one of his best men, Bill Peyto, as head guide. Peyto took
Whymper and four Swiss guides to Emerald Lake. As Whymper later
explained, he had not intended to visit "the Yoho Valley until the end of
the season, as, having been informed that trails were going to be cut, I
proposed to wait until they were made, and to take advantage of them;
but, as at the latter part of July it seemed doubtful if they would be ready
in time, I changed my plans, and decided to go in at once, and to make
our own trails."[20]

Whymper's men finished cutting the trail from Emerald Lake to
Yoho Pass then veered west to cut a trail from the pass to the Little Yoho
Valley (today's Iceline Trail).

They followed a course high on the side of the mountain, parallel
to the Yoho Valley and close to the foot of the Emerald Glacier. After
about a half mile (0.8 kilometres) of heavy cutting, the work became
relatively easy. So much so that they did not anticipate the steep valley
they encountered perpendicular to the trail they were cutting. They
descended into today's Little Yoho Valley and set up camp in the
meadow across from today's Alpine Club of Canada hut. By this time,
Peyto, who was not about to have anyone tell him what to do, especially
when it came to the work of head guide, was thoroughly exasperated
with Whymper's air of superiority. He used two sick horses as an excuse
to depart prematurely for Banff.

Yoho Lake at Yoho Pass, with Wapta Mountain
in the background.

A portion of the Iceline Trail in June 2003. The trail is high above the treeline and retains snow until late in the season. It offers spectacular views of the Yoho Valley below.

Meanwhile, Whymper walked back to Field, where Tom Wilson replaced Peyto with Tom Martin. Wilson himself joined Whymper in the Little Yoho Valley later that summer and tried unsuccessfully to find a shorter route back to Field over Kiwetinok Pass (see Route I on page 53). At one point Whymper was camped alongside Professor Hammond (see pages 97–101), who commented that "Mr. Whymper … seemed greatly impressed with the grandeur and immensity of our Canadian Rockies."[21]

Although he was well past his prime as a climber, was drinking heavily, and could not get along with the men working for him, Whymper did manage to photograph most of the mountains in the Little Yoho Valley, provide some publicity for the railroad, and accomplish a significant amount of trail cutting.

His most memorable contribution, however, was probably suggesting the Burgess Pass route to the Yoho Valley. Though McArthur had climbed Burgess Pass in 1892, this potential route to the Yoho Valley had not been used since. Whymper proposed that a trail be cut over Burgess Pass and along the slopes of Wapta Mountain to Yoho Pass. The CPR cut the trail (today's Wapta Highline trail) in 1901. Despite the fact that the ascent from Field to Burgess Pass is very steep, this was a commonly used alternative route to the Yoho Valley until 1909, when the road up the Yoho River was completed. Although it is unlikely that Whymper knew of it, his Wapta Highline trail probably contributed indirectly to the most important fossil discovery in the world, the Burgess Shale fossils (see pages 118–126). The Walcott family discovered this fossil bed only a short distance from the trail, while traversing the route.

Another Whymper trail, to Yoho Lake, provided an entry point to Yoho Valley for a unique group of tourists. On August 26, 1901, the Vaux family, whom Jimmy Simpson had accompanied to Emerald Lake two years earlier, returned to visit Takakkaw Falls. Though a large group of men was still working on the trail,[22] they managed to reach their destination, making Mary Vaux the first non-Aboriginal woman to see the Yoho Valley. Some ten years later, Mary wrote to Charles Walcott:

> Thee knows I feel a sense of ownership in [the Yoho Valley], being the first white woman that visited it, and besides I have come passed it on the high levels, going in from Sherbrooke Lake, and making a complete circuit over the snow fields and glaciers as well as making the approach from Bow Lake over the Bow Glacier, by Vulture Col, and Balfour Glacier, and across Yoho Glacier to the Valley. It is to me the loveliest spot to be found, and it always quickens my blood when I hear and speak of it, and I can imagine no greater delight than camping there away from the tourist, and the noise of the iron horse.[23]

In September 1901, the trail to Emerald Lake saw its first two-legged nighttime travellers. Mountaineer James Outram later described the unusual endeavour:

> Crossing the river, we had an easy mile along the flat to the beginning of the woods, into which we turned in absolute darkness, save for the glimmer of our lantern.... [W]e followed the little trail, plunging through the darkness and the mud, until a gleam of water shot through the densely growing trees, and in a few moments we stood beside the lake.[24]

Outram and his brother spent the rest of the night at the log huts, then followed the trail along the lake, across the gravel flats, and up to Yoho Pass and Lake. They proceeded to the Takakkaw Falls viewpoint, then chose an alpine route to return to Field.

The Emerald Lake and Yoho Valley trails saw a number of noteworthy visitors over the following few years. In 1904 the British Museum commissioned Mrs. Mary de la Beach-Nichol, a sixty-year-old Welsh adventurer, to study the moths and butterflies of the Canadian Rockies. After raising six children, Beach-Nichol had turned her attention to lepidoptera; her substantial means allowed her to develop a collection that ranked her with such renowned collectors as the Rothschilds.

Beach-Nichol hired Jimmy Simpson, who had left Wilson's employ to start his own outfitting operation, to guide her. Simpson rode, as guides normally did, and Beach-Nichol was joined on her walk into Emerald Lake by botanist John Macoun, who was on a government assignment to update the collection of the local museum.[25] They parted ways at Emerald Lake, where Beach-Nichol checked into the recently built Emerald Lake Chalet. Macoun carried on to Twin Falls and camped near the Yoho Glacier. He later moved back to Takakkaw Falls, then to Field.

Beach-Nichol was not the only adventurous woman to en-joy the region that summer. Noted Canadian mountain climber

Henrietta Tuzo Wilson travelled on horseback through the Yoho Valley that summer with her brother, Jack. Mary Schäffer hired Tom Wilson to take her on a three-day "conditioning" trip to the Yoho Valley in preparation for longer forays into the wilderness. And Schäffer's friends, the Vauxes, returned to the Yoho Valley – this time with George Vaux's future wife, Mary James. Mary Vaux, however, only got as far as Emerald Lake, where she stayed behind with her ailing father.

Another notable visitor that summer was Winnipeg's Elizabeth Parker, one of the founding members of the Alpine Club of Canada. Parker was neither a mountain climber nor a backcountry traveller. She did, however, spend some time in Banff for health reasons, and as part of that stay took a trail ride to Yoho Pass and the viewpoint overlooking Takakkaw Falls. The party returned to Field over the newly built Burgess Pass trail, no doubt grateful that Whymper had suggested it.

In July 1906 Parker was among the 112 alpine enthusiasts who visited Summit (Yoho) Lake for the first annual camp of the newly formed Alpine Club of Canada. Participants left Field on foot, crossed the gravel flats of the Kicking Horse River, then followed the CPR's Emerald River trail to the lake. In spite of its popularity, "The forest trail to Emerald Lake was cool, quiet, scented with the pines which formed a cathedral aisle; at its head a noble peak lifted its glistening crown of snow onto an intensely blue sky."[26] On Habel's old trail across the gravel flats at the end of Emerald Lake, amateur botanist Julia Henshaw was delighted to find thick clumps of "… the large Yellow Lady's Slipper (*Cypripedium pubescens*) in all its rare perfection."[27]

The party forded the endless streams flowing over the gravel flats from Emerald Glacier, then ascended the steep cliff wall that appeared to block further progress until "at last, that striking picture of a tented town nestling amid the realm of trees!"[28] All the baggage had been transported to the site by pack horses, guided by skilled outfitters who had volunteered their services.

Elizabeth Parker (1856–1944)

Although Elizabeth Parker never climbed a mountain, she is best known in the Rockies as a co-founder of the Alpine Club of Canada (ACC). With the 1931 ACC decision to name the very popular Lake O'Hara hut in her honour, her name stays fresh in the minds of mountain travellers.

Parker was born to George and Mary Tupper in Colchester County, Nova Scotia, on December 19, 1856. She attended Normal School in Truro and taught for a year before marrying Henry Parker at age eighteen. The young couple moved to Halifax, where their three children were born. In 1892 they relocated to Winnipeg; Elizabeth subsequently began working for the *Manitoba Free Press*.

In 1904 deteriorating health pushed her farther west. Hoping that the clear mountain air and healing effects of the hot springs would cure her, Parker moved to Banff. She stayed for eighteen months, becoming, in her own words, a "mountain pilgrim."[29]

Upon her return to Winnipeg, she wrote a series of articles urging Canadians to become aware of the national asset held in their mountain heritage. Some time later, a copy of A.O. Wheeler's *The Selkirk Range* crossed her desk. In it, Wheeler proposed forming a Canadian chapter of the American Alpine Club, arguing that initiating a Canadian club was not feasible.

Parker was incensed. She soundly rebuked him, writing in the *Manitoba Free Press*: "We owe it to our own young nationhood, in simple self-respect, to begin an organized system of mountaineering on an independent basis.... It is simply

Winnipeg journalist Elizabeth Parker was a key driving force in the founding of the Alpine Club of Canada. The very popular ACC hut at Lake O'Hara is named in her honour.

amazing that for so long we have cared so little."[30] Recognizing that Parker had "declaimed my action as unpatriotic, chided my lack of imperialism, and generally gave me a pen-lashing in words sharper than a sword,"[31] Wheeler nonetheless accepted the criticism.

The two began working together, and on March 27, 1906, were able to hold the founding meeting of the ACC in Winnipeg. Wheeler was elected president, Parker secretary, and her daughter Jean librarian. Parker's involvement with the ACC was lifelong. She attended every camp until 1913, when her health no longer permitted her to travel, and wrote many articles for the *Canadian Alpine Journal*. She died in 1944 at the age of eighty-eight.

During the eight days of this first-ever ACC camp, club members took trips to various sites around the Yoho Valley. One of the most popular was a two-day circle trip following Habel's route to the valley floor, Wilson's route past Takakkaw Falls and Twin Falls, and Whymper's upper trail from the Little Yoho Valley back to camp. In all, sixty people took the tour, with pack horses carrying the food and baggage. Some participants extended these circular trips to the edge of the Yoho Glacier in order to set out a series of metal plates to measure its recession.

En route, they met up with George and Mary Vaux, who had been camped nearby as part of their own glacial studies. When the camp broke up on July 16, many participants followed the Wapta Highline trail past the yet to be discovered Burgess Shale beds and over Burgess Pass to Field.

Outfitter packing supplies and equipment from Field to Emerald Lake and over Yoho Pass into the ACC camp at Yoho Lake.

The Emerald Lake Road saw further history in the making at the end of the 1907 season. Returning from their four-month adventure along the North Saskatchewan and Athabasca rivers, Mary Schäffer and her companions had crossed Howse and Amiskwi passes (see page 53) to the Emerald Lake Road, which they were following to Field. Travelling in the opposite direction was a carriage carrying a well-dressed couple who turned out to be none other than Rudyard Kipling and his wife, Carrie. Always embarrassed to meet up with city folk when she was still dressed in backcountry garb, Schäffer was exceptionally so this time.

Kipling recorded his version of the encounter in his *Letters of Travel (1892-1913)*:

> As we drove along the narrow hill-road a piebald pack pony with a china-blue eye came round a bend followed by two women, black-haired, bare-headed, wearing beadwork squaw jackets and riding straddle.... A string of pack-ponies trotted through the pines behind them. 'Indians on the move?' said I. 'How characteristic!' As the women jolted by, one of them very slightly turned her eyes, and they were, past any doubt, the comprehending equal eyes of the civilized white woman which moved in that berry-brown face.... The same evening, at a hotel of all the luxuries, a slight woman in a very pretty evening frock was turning over photographs, and the eyes beneath the strictly-arranged hair were the eyes of the woman in the beadwork jacket who had quirted the piebald pack-pony past our buggy. Praised be Allah for the diversity of his creatures![32]

Opposite above: The 1906 ACC camp at Summit (Yoho) Lake. This was the club's first annual camp. A large number of tents were required to shelter the camp's 112 participants. Somehow the environment survived.

Opposite below: The spot (in 2003) where the tongue of the Yoho Glacier would have been in 1906.

Participants in the Alpine Club of Canada's 1909 camp used an alternate route to reach the Yoho Valley. The camp was held at Lake O'Hara, but having experienced the Yoho Valley's splendour at their 1906 camp, many participants could not resist its appeal. After the official end of the 1909 camp, a group of thirty-three members chose to extend their sojourn by undertaking a high-level circuit of the Yoho Valley, beginning at Sherbrooke Lake. This is the trip Mary Vaux refers to in her 1912 letter to Charles Walcott (see page 107). While the trip itself was not very successful, largely due to poor organization,[33] at least one participant claimed that Mary's "cheerfulness in putting up with the little inconveniences of camp life and readiness to give a hand wherever needed, charmed all, and contributed much to the pleasure of the trip."[34]

Later in 1909, CPR publicist John Murray Gibbon embarked upon his first outfitted trip in the Rockies. He and his friend Frank Carrell, editor of the *Quebec Telegraph*, met guide Tom Wilson and his horses at the CPR's Field station. They followed the well-travelled road to Emerald Lake and on past Yoho Pass to set up camp at the lookout overlooking Takakkaw Falls. They then followed Whymper's Skyline Trail to the Little Yoho Valley and on to the Yoho Glacier. They returned to Field along another route pioneered by Whymper: the Wapta Highline and Burgess Pass trails, effectively completing a figure-eight circuit of the Emerald Lake/Yoho Valley region.

(l–r) CPR publicist John Murray Gibbon with palaeontologist Charles Walcott and outfitter Tom Wilson.

The Burgess Shale

In the early twentieth century, Habel's route to Yoho Valley from Emerald Lake over Yoho Pass was the main access route to the Yoho and Little Yoho Valleys. But construction of a road along Tom Wilson and Jim Wright's 1884 route up the Yoho River had begun in 1904. Following its 1909 completion, tourists no longer had to spend a full day to reach the Yoho Valley via Yoho or Burgess pass. A single hour's ride from Field would get them right to the falls. Once completed, this road supplanted much of the trail use over Yoho Pass.

The Yoho Valley Road significantly increased tourist traffic to the valley. This effect pales, however, in comparison with the impact it was to have on modern science. The single most important ramification of having a road into the Yoho Valley was the discovery of the Burgess Shale beds and subsequent quarrying and transporting of shale samples to the railway.

Dr. Charles Doolittle Walcott, self-taught geologist and palaeontologist and secretary of the Smithsonian Institution in Washington, DC, first came to the Canadian Rockies in the summer of 1907. His travels were largely dictated by science, his primary goals being to study geology and to collect fossils.

Near the end of the summer of 1909, Walcott; his wife, Helena; daughter, Helen; son Stuart; and helper/camp manager Arthur Brown, moved camp from the Laggan (Lake Louise) area to Field. The entire party – along with packer Jack Giddie – rode up the recently completed Yoho Valley Road to Takakkaw Falls and pitched their tent. The next day, Walcott took two horses to a spot near Burgess Pass and set up camp. The rest of the group followed. Little did they know that August 31, 1909, was to go down in history as the first time the Burgess Shale beds – possibly the single most important fossil find in the world – drew scientific attention.[35]

Opposite above: The Yoho Valley Road as it appeared early in the twentieth century.

Opposite below: Today's trail leading over Yoho Pass from Emerald Lake.

DR. CHARLES DOOLITTLE WALCOTT (1850–1927)

Charles Walcott was born in New York Mills, New York, on March 31, 1850. His father died two years later; when he was seven, his mother moved the family to nearby Utica, New York. Young Walcott had trouble with teachers in grammar school and dropped out of Utica Academy before graduation. He never went to college. Yet despite his lack of formal education, he became a world-famous scientist and went on to receive many honorary doctorates.

His interest in fossils developed very early on. Through the friendship of local farmer William Rust, he had gained a good knowledge of fossils by the age of sixteen. He later moved to the Rust farm and married Rust's younger sister, who died of natural causes two years later. Walcott made the transition from collector of fossils to palaeontologist, publishing his first four papers in 1875. Later that year, he was fortunate to obtain employment with geologist and palaeontologist James Hall. His work with Hall led to a job with the United States Geological Survey (USGS) in 1879.

By 1891 Walcott was world famous for his geological studies with the USGS; he was named director of the USGS in 1894. Even as director, he managed to be in the field almost every season. He was a workaholic engaged in never-ending scientific work and constantly publishing scientific papers. Walcott is also said to have been involved in almost every aspect of American scientific policy, yet he somehow managed to be a family man as well. He married Helena Stevens in June 1888 and had four children over the next seven years.

Walcott received his first honorary doctorate in 1898; in January 1907, his scientific work took a change in direction when he was elected secretary (head) of the prestigious Smithsonian

Dr. Charles Doolittle Walcott, the man who brought the Burgess Shale fossils to the world's attention. He mined huge quantities of fossil-bearing shale and shipped it to the Smithsonian Institution in Washington, DC.

Institution in Washington, DC. As head of the USGS, his mandate had been the United States; his new position allowed him to extend his studies northward. Later that year, he took his first trip to Canada – specifically to the town of Field, in Yoho National Park.

Walcott and his family spent the entire summer camping and travelling in the Canadian Rockies nearly every year for the rest of his life. In 1909 his family discovered the Burgess Shale fossil beds, the most important fossil discovery ever made. He travelled widely throughout the Rockies, studying geology and collecting fossils, always using his own horses for travelling and spending his summers in tents. There are few, if any, major trails he did not follow.

As successful as Walcott's working life was, his personal life was rather tragic. After having lost his first wife to disease, his second wife, Helena, the mother of his children, was killed in a train accident in July 1911. His son Charlie died in April 1913 and his son Stuart died in France in December 1917. One positive aspect of Walcott's personal life during this later period was his marriage to Mary Vaux in June 1914. She easily fit in with his pattern of life divided between the Rockies and Washington and was a constant companion during his later years.

Walcott had intended to resign from the Smithsonian Institution in June of 1927. However, he died of a stroke in February of that year, two years after his last field trip to the Canadian Rockies.

Unfortunately, there is no first-hand documentation of how this future (1980) World Heritage Site was discovered. Walcott's official report stated that "a most interesting discovery of unique Cambrian fossils was made near Burgess Pass."[36] Several stories relating the discovery have been circulated. None can be authenticated, and some are simply false. One comes to us through a report daughter Helen wrote for her granddaughter in 1955 when she was sixty-one years old: "Father and Mother were returning to camp one day, by way of Burgess Pass. Father wanted to see an outcrop on the base of the cliffs on Mt. Wapta, so mother waited on the trail while father made the steep climb up the scree. She began to split open the shale by the side of the trail, and by the time father returned she had several very remarkable fossils."[37]

If this is correctly recalled, Helena Walcott is the one who actually discovered the Burgess Shale deposits. Although Charles Walcott has been credited with the discovery, he never claimed to have made it, nor did he ever say who did!

Over the next four years, Walcott's summers followed a set pattern. He, as many family members as could make it, and their faithful employee Arthur Brown – an excellent packer whom the family considered the best camp cook in the world – would leave Washington as early as possible in the summer, generally late June or early July.

Once in the Rockies, they headed straight for the quarry – probably along the same trail through the Yoho Valley, over Yoho Pass, and along the Wapta Highline they had used to find the quarry. While J.J. McArthur's Burgess Pass route would have shortened the journey – and did become quite popular among other visitors hiking or riding to the quarry – Walcott does not mention using it. It may be that it was too steep for heavily laden pack horses. However they got there, the Walcotts would spend between four and six weeks near Burgess Pass, quarrying rock and shipping it off to Washington, before extending their travels – and studies – to other parts of the Rocky Mountains.

Walcott's 1910 report paints a picture of life at the quarry:

> Have been putting every available hour into collecting and necessary work of camp. Mrs. Walcott is enjoying the collecting & and is now breaking up rock for 'lace crabs'.... If weather permits we will work the locality very thoroughly – It

is 1200 feet [366 metres] up the mountain side from camp in a broken cliff & debris slope. We have to dig out places to stand & sit in. Have a supply of dynamite, etc. & will attack the beds *in situ* as soon as the blocks on the slopes are worked up. The boys are strong & active & we take down slabs of the richest rock for Mrs. Walcott to split up. Helen & Arthur look after camp. Jack Giddie the packer is kept busy looking after the horses – going out for supplies to Field, etc.[38]

Samples were brought down the mountain to camp, then transported to the railway in Field by pack train. In some years as many as nineteen horses, two quarrymen, and two packers were needed to complete the task.

In July of 1911, tragedy interrupted these idyllic family sojourns: Helena Walcott died in a Connecticut train crash. Somehow, quarrying carried on as usual at the Burgess Shale that summer, but the following year, Walcott spent only two weeks at the quarry. He spent most of the summer in the Mount Robson area, though he did return to the quarry in late September.

Walcott also found time that summer to meet with Mary Vaux and go for a walking tour of one of the glaciers that she was studying. Walcott had first met Vaux, her brother George, and his wife Mary, on his first trip to the Rockies. They met up again at the Laggan hotel in 1909, at which point Charles introduced his wife, Helena, to the family.[39] The Vaux family, who had been coming to the area since the 1880s, would take on increasing significance in Walcott's life. On June 30, 1914, the twice-married sixty-four-year-old Walcott married the independent-minded spinster Mary Vaux one month short of her fifty-fifth birthday.

For the first time in six years, Walcott did not visit the quarry during the summer of 1914. Instead, he and Mary spent their summer measuring glaciers. They returned to the old Burgess Pass camp in 1917 and spent two months quarrying the shale. On September 10 he reported:

Helen Breese Walcott, daughter of Charles and Helena Walcott, wrote that it was her mother who actually discovered the first Burgess Shale fossil beds.

fossils & a number of slabs. A good collection but the quarry is played out."[40] Though the Walcotts did spend a month collecting fossils at the Burgess Pass camp two years later, the summer of 1917 was the last time Walcott devoted significant time and effort to the work.

MARY VAUX WALCOTT (1860–1940)

The Walcott Quarry today, looking east. The site appears rather underwhelming considering its importance to world science.

MARY VAUX WALCOTT (1860–1940)

Mary Vaux was the eldest of three children born to a Philadelphia Quaker family. She had a keen interest in drawing and painting, a fascination with scientific pursuits, a passion for mountain climbing, and a strong love of travel.

However, throughout most of her life, her activities were curtailed by family circumstances. Following her mother's death in 1880, Vaux was expected to keep house for her father and brothers. At a time when most young women were thinking mainly about marriage, Vaux was burdened with the task of both running the family home in Philadelphia and the summer home near Bryn Mawr – including the dairy farm – which she ran until 1922.

The family began travelling west in 1885. They first explored Yellowstone National Park and the California coast, but in 1887 they ended their trip with an excursion to the Canadian Rockies. They spent most of their time at Glacier House in Rogers Pass, where they began measuring the Illecillewaet Glacier. They returned in 1894, and Vaux spent nearly every summer for the next forty years in the region. The glacier studies continued – first with both brothers, later with one, then on her own until 1912, when other interests diverted her attention.

In 1900 Vaux climbed Mount Stephen, becoming the first woman to execute a major climb in Canada. Thirteen years later, she was the first woman to climb Mount Robson. Nevertheless, her mountain-climbing feats were few. Her major interests were in the field of botany and botanical art. She was an accomplished wildflower painter and later gained skill as an amateur photographer. Her crowning achievement, however, was having her wildflower paintings used to illustrate the Smithsonian's five volumes of *North American Wild Flowers*.

Mary Vaux Walcott, the first woman to visit the Yoho Valley, spent most summers of her adult life in the Canadian Rockies.

Vaux met Dr. Charles Walcott, secretary of the Smithsonian Institution, and his wife, Helena, at the hotel on Lake Louise in the summer of 1909. No one could have guessed that in 1911 Helena would die in a tragic train accident and that three years later, one month short of her fifty-fifth birthday, Mary Vaux would become Walcott's third wife. Her father was very upset by the wedding and would not attend. Vaux moved to Washington, where she lived for the rest of her life. Her father died one year later.

Despite an inauspicious start, the Walcotts had a very happy life together, becoming real soulmates. Walcott's pattern of spending the entire summer camping in the Canadian Rockies while carrying out his scientific studies suited his new wife perfectly. In the early years of their marriage, Charles helped her with her glacier studies. Later, she devoted her attention to her wildflower studies.

From her earliest days in the Rockies, Vaux had a special affinity for the Yoho Valley; she camped and explored throughout its entirety. With the Burgess Shale quarry on the side of Mount Field in Yoho National Park, and access through the Yoho Valley, her time there only increased after her marriage.

Following Charles's death in 1927, Mary continued her trips to the Rockies until 1939. The main difference was that she now drove to the West in a chauffeured car. She continued to attend the annual camps of the Alpine Club of Canada and the annual rides of the Trail Riders of the Canadian Rockies, where she was often referred to as the "Grand Dame" of the Canadian Rockies. Throughout her life she was very active in various organizations in Philadelphia, Washington, and her Canadian summer home. She died of a heart attack in 1940 at a friend's home in St. Andrews-by-the-Sea, New Brunswick. She was eighty years old.

CHANGING TIMES

As travel in the National Parks became more popular, federal authorities had begun to take more interest in maintaining the trails and keeping track of where people were going and what they were doing. In 1911, before the Warden Service was formalized, the park was patrolled by federal forest rangers. The following year, a single Yoho Park warden patrolled from Field to Emerald Lake and on to the Yoho River, as well as several other trails outside the Yoho Valley. In 1913 one warden was responsible for thirty-three miles (fifty-three kilometres) along five trails leading out of Field toward Takakkaw Falls, Emerald Lake, the Burgess Pass, the Burgess Shale fossil beds, and the Ottertail Fire Road. Another patrol route began at Takakkaw Falls and led to Twin Falls, Yoho Glacier, Summit Lake, and back to Takakkaw Falls, twenty-one miles (thirty-four kilometres) in all.[41]

In spite of the large quarry the Walcotts created on the ridge between Wapta Mountain and Mount Field and the many tons of fossil-laden rock samples they shipped to the United States, there is no mention of ever having had a permit for this work. It seems that the government of the time was not concerned about people of any nationality removing rock from a National Park. Even on September 22, 1913, when a game warden visited the Walcotts' camp to discuss a permit issued for hunting and collecting animals for scientific purposes, there was no mention of the removal of fossils.

In the summer of 1916, the Warden Service expanded its range of duties by clearing deadfall from the trail from Takakkaw Falls to Twin Falls, the Yoho Glacier trail, the upper trail from Twin Falls back to Yoho Lake and down to Takakkaw Falls, the Wapta Highline trail from Yoho Lake to Burgess Pass, and the Burgess Pass trail down to Field.[42]

Their efforts facilitated the work of portrait artist J.S. Sargent, who spent part of the summer of 1916 in the Yoho Valley. He arrived in Field on August 2 and immediately began arranging supplies and guides for an expedition up the Yoho Valley Road and on to Twin Falls. On August 20, he wrote his friend Mrs. Gardner:

> I am camping under the waterfall that Mr. Denman Ross gave me a postcard of. It is magnificent when the sun shines

which it did the first two days. I began a picture – that is ten days ago – and since then it has been raining and snowing steadily – provisions and temper getting low – but I shall stick it out till the sun reappears. Tell Mr. Ross that he was quite right, but that now there is only one fall of the 'Twins,' thanks to some landslip above.[43]

By August 28 Sargent had returned to Mount Stephen House. On August 30 he wrote his cousin, Mary Hale:

It was raining and snowing, my tent flooded, mushrooms sprouted in my boots, porcupines taking shelter in my clothes, canned food always fried in a black frying pan getting on my nerves, and a fine waterfall which was the attraction of the place pounding and thundering all night. I stood it for three weeks and yesterday came away with a repulsive picture.[44]

Sargent's picture was a painting of Twin Falls, but since one fall was blocked, he painted only the bottom of the fall and titled the painting *Yoho Falls*.

More favourable conditions appear to have greeted the famous Group of Seven painter Lawren Harris when he visited the Emerald Lake/Yoho Valley area in 1924. Harris painted around Emerald Lake, Takakkaw Falls, and the Waterfall Valley near Twin Falls. There he painted Mont des Poilus, which dominates the view of this valley noted for its solitude and abundance of wildlife.[45]

There was little solitude to be had early that July when Caroline Hinman used the Yoho Valley Road and trails as a warm-up for a group of eighteen vacationers and six men who were to look after their needs (see Route I on pages 58–60). They spent the first night just past Takakkaw Falls, probably where the campground is now. "The next day [they] rode up to Twin Falls but one twin had run dry."[46] They rode on to the flats at the end of Emerald Lake, where they spent the night. From there they proceeded to the Natural Bridge and on along the

Amiskwi River. In retrospect, Hinman's party of approximately forty horses may have been very quiet compared to a normal July day today near Emerald Lake.

But signs of the region's future were already present around Takakkaw Falls in the early 1920s. By 1922 three-day trail rides like Gibbon's 1909 excursion had become so popular that the CPR expanded its 1906 tent camp near Takakkaw Falls to a bungalow camp that could accommodate thirty-six guests. There, Banff's Brewster Brothers had set up an operation supplying horses and guides for trail rides. Gerry Andrews, who spent the summer of 1919 as cook at the tent camp, wrote:

> More affluent and leisurely guests took a three-day trip by saddle horse with guides. First day was by trail over Burgess and Yoho Passes to overnight at the camp. Second day featured the trail up to the head of Yoho Valley to see the ice cave and other sights there and back to the camp for a second night. Day three was by trail over Yoho Pass and down to Emerald Lake Chalet, thence to Field by road.[47]

It was at this bungalow camp that Charles Walcott spent his last days in the Yoho Valley. The camp provided some comfort to a sick and elderly man (see page 118–126

Meanwhile Gibbon himself had been hooked on trail riding;[48] what appeared at first glance to be a very ordinary three-day trail ride around Yoho Valley turned out to have long-lasting effects for mountain travellers. In 1923, while riding along the Rockwall in what is today Kootenay National Park, he and a group of friends conceived the idea of the Trail Riders of the Canadian Rockies. This group, inaugurated under the auspices of the CPR, organized several trail rides through the Rockies each summer. As with Caroline Hinman's Off the Beaten Track tours, participants were recruited through advertising and did not normally know one another prior to the excursion. Though no longer affiliated with the railway, the Trail Riders organization still exists today.

Fittingly enough, the Trail Riders' inaugural ride began at Field, with the first night's camp set up near Takakkaw Falls.[49] The association's executive had decided to mark the occasion with an acknowledgement of Tom Wilson's historic contribution to trail riding. They commissioned a bronze plaque featuring his image and the words: "Tom Wilson/ Trailblazer of the Canadian Rockies/Lake Louise 1882/Emerald Lake 1882," which they erected on a large stone at the entrance to Yoho Valley. Two hundred and seven alpine enthusiasts – including Wilson himself – were present at the unveiling. The plaque remained in the valley until Wilson's death in 1933, when it was moved to mark his grave in the Old Banff Cemetery.[50]

The Walcotts' 1924 return to the Burgess Shale demonstrates how quickly times had changed. As usual, they travelled to Field by train. From there, however, they were conveyed to a bungalow camp at Takakkaw Falls

Tom Wilson with the Yoho Valley plaque at its unveiling. The plaque now marks his grave in the Old Banff Cemetery.

by motor car. The horses and camping gear arrived next day, allowing the Walcotts to proceed to their old Burgess Pass camp. But the only work Walcott – now seventy-four years old – was able to do was collect fossils from around the campsite.

After about a week, he and Mary returned to Takakkaw Falls for the Trail Riders' first outing and the plaque unveiling. Having travelled more recorded miles on horseback in the mountains than any other person, Walcott had been named honorary president of the organization. He estimated his travels thus:

> I have traced on the map the principal trails over which I have ridden in connection with geological work.... [W]e made from 18 to 30 camps each season ... averaging 100 days each season ... [w]hich would give 780 days at a minimum average of five miles [eight kilometres] per day. This is in addition to the riding in connection with moving from camp to camp.[51]

The day after the unveiling ceremony, the Trail Riders moved up the valley to a new rest house at Twin Falls, which the CPR had built that year as part of their efforts to provide facilities for tourists travelling in the mountains. They returned along the upper trail, much as Wilson and Gibbon had done fifteen years earlier.

The outing was to be Walcott's last sojourn in the Yoho Valley. On July 18, he sent the pack train to Lake Louise and moved into a bungalow, where he was ill with stomach problems. He was soon well enough to resume travel. He and Mary spent the remainder of the summer studying geology and collecting fossils throughout the mountains. They left for the east on September 26, 1924.

One final season in the Rockies followed, after which Walcott reported: "Mrs. Walcott and I returned from our fieldwork in the Canadian Rockies, full of the joy of living and ready to take up the duties of the winter."[52] It seems the joy of living was not to be with him much longer. Walcott died in February 1927.

The Trail Today

The Emerald Lake and Yoho Valley regions of Yoho National Park are both serviced by paved roads and are popular destinations for tourists and locals alike. Most trails in these regions of the park are suitable as day hikes for people of all ages. The trails from Emerald Lake to Yoho Pass and the circular route to Burgess Pass and back to Emerald Lake are heavily used, especially by visitors to the Emerald Lake resort. Today the resort is known as the Emerald Lake Lodge and consists of a large number of cabins in addition to the main lodge.

The old Highline and Skyline trails, which approximate Whymper's route to the Little Yoho Valley, were also popular routes until 1987, when the Iceline Trail was built along moraines from the receding glacier. Environmental concerns led to partial closure of the former two trails in 1990.

Wilson's trail up the Yoho Valley was rarely used until the road to Takakkaw Falls was completed in 1909, but it now provides easy access to the falls for thousands of tourists a year. The trail that continues from the end of the road at Takakkaw Falls on to Twin Falls and beyond is heavily used today. All of the trails in this area of Yoho National Park have bridges across the streams, so no fords are required.

Beautiful scenery abounds throughout the area and there are five hike-in campsites for those who would like a longer stay. Entering the area on the trail Tom Wilson used when he went looking for his horses offers a very peaceful walk through the forest and along the Emerald River, with very little change in elevation. The trail from Emerald Lake to the end of the gravel flats is again fairly flat and very scenic.

A short distance from the beginning of the trail around the lake is a large avalanche path that brings snow and other debris thundering down from the slopes of Emerald Peak into the lake. I was fortunate enough to experience the remains of one of these massive avalanches when I visited the lake in mid-June 2000. The trail was covered in several metres of heavy, hard-packed snow for some distance, and the toe of the avalanche had advanced well out into the lake. The source of the avalanche was not visible from lake level, but it was very evident from the top of Burgess Pass, looking toward the lake.

From the end of the lake, the route first recorded by Habel is a short, steep climb to the top of Yoho Pass. The alluvial fan at the end of Emerald Lake is well known for its abundance of yellow lady's slippers in late June and July. They were in full bloom on June 24, 2004, when my wife, Cheryl, and I hiked the trail, even though snow was still heavy on Yoho Pass.

Yoho Lake is a pretty little lake surrounded by trees that offers a good view of Wapta Mountain in the background. From here the trail drops steeply down to the parking area near Takakkaw Falls. To do this hike in reverse involves a short, steep hike to Yoho Lake from the parking area, suitable for most hikers.

From Takakkaw Falls, the hike to the gravel flats near where Habel observed the cave at the tongue of the Yoho Glacier in 1900 involves only a very gradual climb on a good trail. There are many side trips that

The remains of a massive avalanche that swept down the side of Emerald Peak and into Emerald Lake on June 9, 2000. Note the people walking on the tongue, on June 13.

can be taken from this trail. In 1975 I hiked this trail with Cheryl, going as far as the junction to the Yoho Glacier, then turning west to Twin Falls. In fact, the co-author was also along on this trip; she was born about two months after her mother took the hike!

Beginning at Field, one can also access Yoho Lake by taking the Burgess Pass trail first hiked by surveyor J.J. McArthur. However, the unrelenting steep climb to the top of the pass will only appeal to a small number of people. For those who make it that far, however, the scenery along the sides of Mount Field and Wapta Mountain en route to Yoho Lake is well worth the effort.

Most will want to take this trail in the opposite direction, starting at Yoho Lake and thus avoiding the climb to Burgess Pass. The Walcott Quarry, on the slopes between Mount Field and Wapta Mountain, is accessed from this trail. Because the quarry is now protected as the Burgess Shales World Heritage Site, it is carefully monitored by remote cameras and other means. Access is permitted only by guided tours offered by the Yoho Burgess Shale Foundation. These tours begin at the Takakkaw Falls parking lot, climb to Yoho Lake, and follow along the base of Wapta Mountain to the trail leading to the quarry, the same route Walcott first used in 1909.

From Yoho Lake, hikers can also take the Iceline Trail along the slopes of the President Range, high above the treeline. This trail, most of which follows the moraines of the Emerald Glacier, is higher on the mountain than Whymper's original trail (now closed for environmental reasons). There is very little vegetation along much of the route, but it offers spectacular views over the Yoho Valley and of the Waputik Icefield beyond. The Emerald Glacier is in nearly constant view high above, and at one point, hikers can look down on the top of Takakkaw Falls. The trail is not easy, though, as it involves a significant elevation gain to the top of Iceline Summit. It then drops down to a campground and an Alpine Club hut in the Little Yoho Valley. From there, a short but steep climb leads to the top of Kiwetinok Pass.

Several years ago, the authors and their spouses hiked the Iceline Trail. We camped at the Little Yoho Campground on a cool autumn evening. After supper, a young woman from the next campsite approached us. We discovered that she was visiting from Israel, where she had left temperatures of 35°C. She was not prepared for the cool weather and wondered if we could possibly spare some coffee to warm her up. We were happy to oblige.

Although camping is only allowed in designated campsites, modern backpackers can still put together good loop hikes, just as the Trail Riders did nearly a century ago. Feeling somewhat akin to Caroline Hinman, I once took the circular route with my younger daughter, Susan, and two of her girlfriends. They began at Takakkaw Falls and climbed to the Iceline Trail, which they followed to the Little Yoho Valley, then north to Twin Falls and back along the Yoho River to the starting point.

One night was spent at the Laughing Falls Campground. There were many other campers there and one in particular was very "friendly." The man was my age and was fascinated by the fact that an older man was camping with three very attractive teenaged girls. He first asked if I claimed to be the father of these young ladies. I simply answered no, not offering the information that I was the father of one of them. I felt that he was being nosey and was not inclined to offer a detailed response.

He left but was soon back. He wanted to know if I was a schoolteacher on an outing with some students. He left again after getting a negative answer, but he soon returned with the conclusion that I was the only male Girl Guide leader in Canada. I assured him that I was not. Wearied by his probing, I finally told him that I was simply accompanying my daughter and two of her friends on a backpacking trip, and that I had been taking both daughters and numerous friends, both male and female, on backpacking trips for many years. He did not return.

Trail Guide

Distances are adapted from existing trail guides: Patton and Robinson, Potter, and Beers, and from Gem-Trek maps. Distances intermediate from those given in the sources are estimated from topographical maps and from hiking times. All distances are in kilometres.

From Field over Yoho Pass to the Yoho Glacier

Maps   82 N/7 Golden
               82 N/8 Lake Louise
               82 N/9 Hector Lake
               82 N/10 Blaeberry River
               Lake Louise and Yoho (Gem Trek)

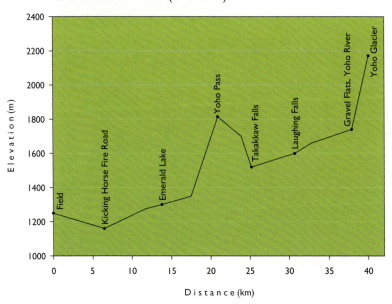

Trailhead

The trail starts at the Burgess Pass trail parking lot. The access road is located 1.2 km northeast of the Field intersection, on the north side of the Trans-Canada Highway. Keep left (west) at the split in the access road and follow it 0.4 km to the parking lot. Using this parking lot avoids having to make a dangerous crossing of the very busy Trans-Canada Highway from Field. There is no access to the trail at the north end.

0.0	Burgess Pass trail parking lot. Follow the Burgess Pass trail west along an old road that initially parallels the highway, then turns sharply uphill into the trees before heading west again.
0.9	Trail junction. The Burgess Pass trail turns sharply to the right (north). Take the minor trail that heads through the forest to the left down toward the highway. At the highway, the trail follows an old roadbed parallel to the highway. This is part of the old motor car road to Emerald Lake. Near Field, the old roadbed disappears into the highway. Continue along the broad right-of-way.
1.9	Rejoin the old roadbed 0.5 km west of Field. The old road initially follows parallel to the highway, then diverges to the north.
4.2	The Tally Ho Trail (a tallyho is a horse-drawn carriage used before the advent of buses) turns to the right to join the Emerald Lake Road. Keep left.
5.0	The trail leads into the Emerald Lake Road and parking lot for the Natural Bridge. Cross the parking lot and follow the Amiskwi Fire Road west along the Kicking Horse River.
6.5	Junction. After crossing the bridge over the Emerald River and before reaching the bridge over the Amiskwi River, turn to the right (north) on the Emerald River trail. The trail is sometimes beside the river, sometimes on a high bank above the river.
8.6	Junction. Old fire road leads to the right (east). There are old footings near the river where there was once a bridge. Continue straight ahead.

9.8 Trail branches. A horse trail goes to the right (east). Continue ahead along the rapidly flowing Emerald River. The trail soon climbs a low ridge, then follows a small creek.

11.7 Cross Russell Creek on a bridge. Continue ahead on a pleasant, well-made trail through light forest.

13.7 Junction. The trail to the left (west) goes to Hamilton Lake. Continue ahead.

13.8 Emerald Lake parking lot. Cross the parking lot to the trailhead sign at the northeast end. Take the paved trail around Emerald Lake to the left (clockwise). The paved trail lasts only a few minutes; continue on the smooth, wide gravel trail with good views of the lake.

15.4 At the alluvial fan at the head of the lake, a trail goes to the left (north) to Emerald Basin. Continue a short distance straight ahead, then turn left (northeast) on a trail leading to Yoho Lake and Yoho Pass. On the alluvial fan there are many branched streams coming down from Emerald Basin, most of them bridged. During spring runoff some of these may be flooded and require fording the stream. Along the way there are wonderful displays of yellow lady's slippers in late June and July. Toward the end of the alluvial fan, a major stream (that is normally bridged) must be crossed.

17.5 Start climbing toward the pass, which appears as a V-notch in the mountains. The trail goes through a series of switchbacks.

18.2 Falls viewpoint. Continue to the top of a ridge, cross a rockfall and continue uphill into the forest.

20.2 Trail junction. The trail to the right (south) goes to Burgess Pass. Continue ahead for Yoho Lake.

20.9 Yoho Lake and trail junction. The trail to the left (north) leads toward the Iceline Trail and Little Yoho Valley. Keep right (southeast) around the lake for Takakkaw Falls.

21.2   The end of the lake. The trail follows the outlet stream from Yoho Lake and enters the forest, offering some good views of the Yoho Valley.

23.2   Directly above Hidden Lakes. There are good views to the south and east across Yoho Valley.

23.9   Junction. The Iceline Trail goes to the left (northwest). Continue to the right (east).

24.1   Junction. The trail to the right (south) goes to Hidden Lake. Continue ahead. The trail starts its steep descent into the Yoho Valley. A series of switchbacks pass through mature forest alternating with an avalanche path to the bottom of the valley.

25.2   Trailhead, hostel parking, and Yoho Valley Road. Cross the road and follow a good trail toward Takakkaw Falls.

25.6   Junction. The trail to the right (northeast) crosses the Yoho River on a bridge. Keep straight ahead. Follow the trail along the river, past the parking areas and the picnic areas to the parking area at the north end.

26.4   Trailhead: the beginning of the trail north along the Yoho Valley.

26.7   Walk-in campground. There is a trail sign at the north end of the campground. The heavily used and well-maintained trail heads north up the valley, first across an alluvial fan, then into light forest.

28.6   Junction. Angels Staircase Falls is on the right (east), Point Lace Falls just ahead on the left (northwest). Continue straight ahead.

30.0   Junction. Duchesnay Lake is to the left (northwest). Continue ahead. Cross the Little Yoho River on a bridge; arrive at Laughing Falls Campground.

30.7   Waterfall on the left. The junction of the trail to the Little Yoho Valley is just beyond the falls, on the left (west). Continue straight ahead and cross Twin Falls Creek on a bridge. The trail climbs away from the creek, then back again to follow it through heavy forest with occasional glimpses of Twin Falls.

32.8   Junction. The trail to Twin Falls Chalet branches to the left (west). Continue to the right (north) toward the Yoho Glacier. The trail climbs steadily through heavy forest, then levels out.

37.3   The trail drops dramatically to above the gravel flats of the Yoho River, then skirts along the side of a rocky moraine above the river.

37.9   Gravel flats. The landscape becomes very rocky and barren. Although this was likely the tongue of the glacier when Habel arrived in 1897, I could not see it in 2005. The access point for the gravel flats is marked by a large cairn. This is the end of the trail as such. To go beyond requires route finding and rock scrambling skills. There is a trail that continues along the edge of the rocky moraine, then veers left (northwest) just beyond the split in the river and starts a long, steep climb on the left (west) side of the river. The trail soon becomes faint and is marked by cairns. With much perseverance, this steep climb reaches the top of a ridge and the river can be followed to the toe of the glacier. I was turned back by a storm at the top of the ridge but spoke with other scramblers who had made it to the glacier.

Today's well-made trail through the Yoho Valley from Takakkaw Falls to near the Yoho Glacier is used by hikers of all ages.

From Field over Burgess Pass to Yoho Lake

Maps   82 N/8 Lake Louise
        Lake Louise and Yoho (Gem Trek)

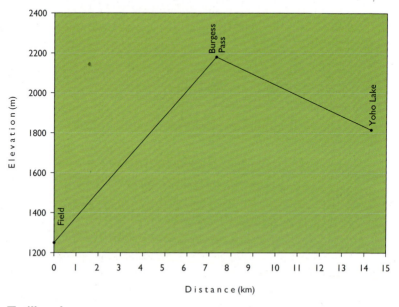

Trailhead

The access road to the Burgess Pass trail parking lot is located 1.2 km northeast of the Field intersection, on the north side of the Trans-Canada Highway. Keep left at the split in the access road and follow it 0.4 km to the parking lot.

0.0   Burgess Pass trail parking lot. Follow the Burgess Pass trail west along an old road that initially parallels the highway, then turns sharply uphill into the trees before heading west again.

0.9   Trail junction. The trail to the left (west) goes to Field; the Burgess Pass trail turns sharply to the right (north). The trail heads straight up the mountain, then levels out before beginning switchbacks (Gem Trek map reports 48).

2.5   Forest thins out, offering views of the town of Field. A short distance farther, the trail criss-crosses a major washout/run-off channel. Continue along fairly steep switchbacks with more frequent views down the Kicking Horse valley.

4.0   Cross an open shale slope, then avalanche slopes. The pass is clearly visible above.

6.4   Trail continues to switchback through the forest, then turns east to avoid a gully.

7.3   Top of the pass. Looking forward, Emerald Lake is visible. A ridge to the left (west) offers good views of the lake. Continue climbing along the summit ridge to the right (east).

7.6   Junction. The trail to the left (north) leads directly to Emerald Lake. Continue to the right (east) toward Yoho Lake. There are good views of both the Kicking Horse valley and Emerald Lake.

9.7   Arrive at a wide open stretch along the slopes of Mount Field. Cross a rock slide area into the trees, then continue on to an open shale slope.

11.4   Begin switchbacks through open areas with good views. At the end of an avalanche path, re-enter the forest. You will soon arrive at another avalanche path. Continue with fabulous views, sheer cliffs on the right (east).

13.3   Enter mature forest.

13.7   Junction. The trail to the left (west) goes to Emerald Lake. Keep right for Yoho Lake.

14.3   Yoho Lake and trail junction. The trail to the left (north) goes to the Little Yoho Valley, the one to the right (southeast) to Takakkaw Falls.

From Yoho Lake to the Little Yoho Valley and Kiwetinok Pass

Maps   Lake Louise 82 N/8
        Blaeberry River 82 N/10
        Lake Louise and Yoho (Gem Trek)

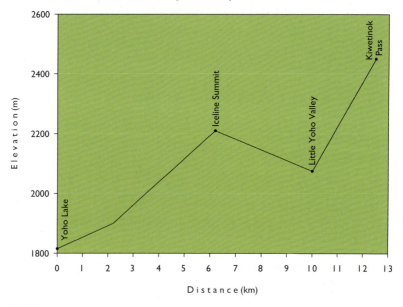

Trailhead

Take the Burgess Pass trail from Field to Yoho Lake, the Yoho Pass trail from Field or Emerald Lake to Yoho Lake, or the trail from Takakkaw Falls to Yoho Lake. All of these trails are described above.

0.0   Trail junction. The trail to the right (southeast) continues along Yoho Lake. Take the Iceline Trail to the left (north). The trail initially climbs through the forest with some switchbacks, then opens out high above Takakkaw Falls with spectacular views of the falls. Cross a large avalanche slope.

2.2   Junction. The trail to the right heads east toward Takakkaw Falls. Keep left on the Iceline Trail. From this junction, the trail starts climbing, sometimes on stairs of rock. Follow high on the side of the President Range, with glaciers constantly in view high above. The trail passes through a glacial moraine with very little vegetation, sometimes marked with cairns. Climbing steadily, it passes two small lakes and crosses small outlet streams, always with great views across the Yoho Valley and beyond.

5.4 Junction. The trail to the right (north) goes to Celeste Lake. Continue straight ahead (northwest), still climbing.

6.2 Iceline Summit. The trail starts a general downhill trend, with the Little Yoho Valley clearly visible from the summit. The trail initially continues on the glacial moraine, then drops down into the trees.

8.1 Trail sign. To the right, the old Highline Trail is closed. Continue to the left on the old Skyline Trail. The trail drops down through the trees, past a massive boulder pile, on to the valley floor and gravel flats with a good view of the Alpine Club hut.

10.0 Junction. The trail to the right (east) crosses the Little Yoho River on a bridge, passes the warden cabin and continues on to the Alpine Club hut and the campground. Keep left (southwest) for Kiwetinok Pass. The trail initially parallels the river, then it passes the campground on the right (north) side of the river and climbs steeply along the side of a narrow canyon to a rocky, barren area. The trail crosses the creek (rock hop), then climbs through trees to a meadow-like area.

10.6 Cross another stream on the rocks. Start the steady climb to the pass through light forest, following close to a creek. Some sections are very steep.

11.3 Above treeline. You will come to a small meadow; continue to climb. When you arrive at a rocky, shale-covered pass, proceed around a rock face to the right (north).

12.2 Kiwetinok Lake. Continue around the lake to the left (west), turn left (west) at the end of a ridge, and continue to climb through rock and shale.

12.5 A sharp drop: the end of the trail. There is a good view down the green, forested valley of the Kiwetinok River, which leads toward the Amiskwi valley.

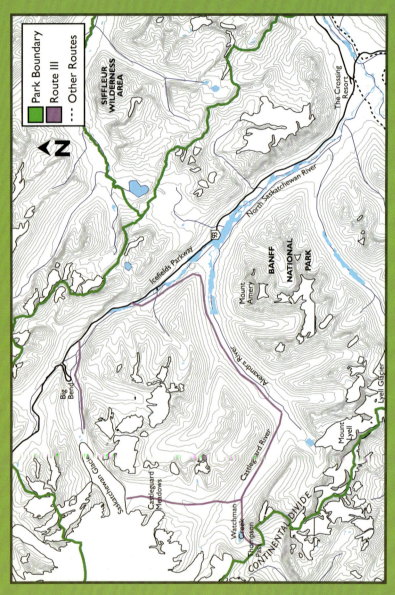

Route III, from the North Saskatchewan River to the Castleguard Meadows, with side trips to the Saskatchewan Glacier.

Park Boundary
Route III
Other Routes

SIFFLEUR
WILDERNESS
AREA

N

The Crossing Resort

North Saskatchewan River

Icefields Parkway

93

BANFF NATIONAL PARK

Mount Amery

Alexandra River

Big Bend

Lyell Glacier

Mount Lyell

Saskatchewan Glacier

Castleguard River

Castleguard Meadows

Watchman Creek

Thompson Pass

CONTINENTAL DIVIDE

Route III

Icy Barrier? Not for the Bold: C.S. Thompson's Route to the Castleguard Valley and Charles Walcott's Route to the Castleguard Meadows

Many years ago, I volunteered to be the adult guide for a group of teenagers who had organized a trip along the Alexandra River and were advertising in the community newspaper for an adult to accompany them. I did not realize they were all members of an army cadet group and were planning on wearing their army fatigues and using army equipment on the trip.

None of this would have caused any problems except that they also felt that army rank and procedures should prevail. I had volunteered to cook for them, as I was accustomed to doing with Janice and her friends when out in the backcountry. The only problem with this arrangement was that at the end of the meal, the cadets simply got up and walked away, leaving me with the dirty dishes. Apparently army cadets – especially cadet officers – do not do cleanup after a meal. The first night, the girls in the group sought to avoid a confrontation by volunteering to do the cleanup, but I was not satisfied with that arrangement on a long-term basis. Strong words were exchanged and some hard feelings developed before each agreed to do his or her share of camp chores. That was my first and last backpacking trip with strangers.

CHRONOLOGY

1896   Walter Wilcox views the Alexandra valley from the shoulder of Mount Saskatchewan.

1900   Mountaineer C.S. Thompson becomes the first known person to visit the Alexandra valley. He continues up the Castleguard River, then follows Watchman Creek to the pass which today bears his name.

1902   Following Thompson's directions, Rev. James Outram crosses Thompson Pass to access Mount Columbia.

1907   Billy Warren and Sid Unwin guide Mary Schäffer and Mollie Adams up the Alexandra and Castleguard rivers and on to Thompson Pass.

1919   The Thompson Pass area sees the arrival of the Inter-provincial Boundary Survey under A.O. Wheeler.

1921   The Walcotts move their geological studies up the Alexandra and Castleguard rivers and on to the Castleguard Meadows, where they set up camp.

        Cecil Smith discovers the Castleguard Caves.

1923   J. Monroe Thorington and Dr. William Ladd hire Jimmy Simpson to escort them to Thompson Pass and the Castleguard Meadows. Simpson makes Rocky Mountain history when he successfully takes his pack train across the Saskatchewan Glacier to Parker Ridge. Shortly after Thorington leaves, the Appalachian Mountaineering Club arrives. After four days, they exit the meadow by Simpson's glacier route.

1924   Members of the Harvard Mountaineering Club make their way to the Castleguard Meadows for an extended stay. They also exit the meadows by taking their horses across the glacier.

Caroline Hinman's Off the Beaten Track tour camps on the Castleguard Meadows in July. They spend time at Thompson Pass, go out onto the glacier, and investigate the cave. They exit along the Alexandra River.

Byron Harmon and Lewis Freeman spend time on the Castleguard Meadows as part of a five-hundred-mile (805-kilometre) trip to Jasper. This party too leaves the area by Simpson's glacier route.

1929   Leopold Amery travels up the Alexandra River to climb the recently named Mount Amery. His party moves on to the Castleguard Meadows for more climbing.

Late   Jack Brewster's Jasper to Lake Louise "Glacier Trail" expeditions
1920s   use the Castleguard Meadows as part of their tour. The venture is devastated by the Depression of the 1930s.

1933   The Castleguard Meadows are part of Cliff and Ruth Kopas's honeymoon trip from southern Alberta to the Pacific Ocean at Bella Coola during the height of the Depression.

Gravel flats near the mouth of the Alexandra River, seen from the Sunset Pass trail. Mount Amery in on the left.

HISTORY

MOUNTAINEERS

The first recorded view of the Alexandra valley took place in 1896.[1] Having climbed a shoulder of Mount Saskatchewan, Walter Wilcox peered down the valley in hopes of discerning whether the Alexandra or the Saskatchewan would lead him to the Athabasca. He perceived the former to be blocked by a glacier and so chose the latter, leaving the Alexandra to enjoy several more years of tranquility.

All along the Continental Divide, mountaineers were viewing remote mountain valleys from adjacent valleys, then exploring them and using them to access other mountains. In 1900, mountaineer C.S. Thompson distinguished himself as the first recorded visitor to the Alexandra valley. Discovering that it was not in fact blocked, he explored to its head, then continued up the Castleguard River. He turned west up Watchman Creek and eventually discovered the pass that was to bear his name.

The valley saw its next visitor in 1902, when Rev. James Outram used information supplied by Thompson and others to access Mount Columbia via Thompson Pass. Outram was an unusual character in that despite his lack of personal funds, he always somehow managed to put together an outfit for his mountaineering exploits. This one was supported by the Canadian Pacific Railway (CPR). The outfit was made up of ten fully laden pack horses, four saddle horses, and nearly a ton (907 kg.) of gear.[2] Swiss guide Christian Kaufmann accompanied the climbers, with Bill Peyto as guide.

The party set out from Banff on July 9. After escorting the group across the North Saskatchewan River, Peyto returned to Banff with three pack horses in order to attend to his outfitting business. At that point, Jimmy Simpson took over as guide, assisted by Fred Ballard.

Rev. James Outram used Thompson Pass to access Mount Columbia, which he successfully climbed.

Having made their home in a small cabin on the Mistaya[3] while they spent the winter trapping in the area, the two men were intimately familiar with the region.

They guided Outram's party up the Alexandra and Castleguard rivers to the gravel flats at the head of the Castleguard, then turned west to cross Thompson Pass. On July 19 they climbed Mount Columbia, some distance west and north of the pass on the Continental Divide. The party returned along the Alexandra River to Glacier Lake, where they joined the party of mountaineer J.N. Collie to do some more climbing. All told, the party was out for fifty-four days and Outram had a very successful summer, participating in ten first ascents.

Opposite: Walter Wilcox (c), the first Caucasian to view the Alexandra valley, spent most
of his life exploring in the Canadian Rockies.
He is shown here with friends, outfitters Jim
Brewster (l) and Tom Wilson (r).

Above: C.S. Thompson (l) with fellow moun-
taineers (l–r): Charles Fay, unknown, Harold
Dixon (seated), unknown, unknown, J. Norman
Collie, Herschel Parker, and Peter Sarbach.

Mary Schäffer and Mollie Adams travelled extensively through the Rocky Mountains for three years until Mollie's untimely death in 1908.

Adventurers

With the highest mountains near the head of the Castleguard River having been climbed, mountaineers seem to have lost interest in the area. Between Outram's first visit to the Castleguard River in 1902 and the 1920s, the only party to visit the area was that of the travelling ladies, Mary Schäffer[4] and Mollie Adams, and their guides Billy Warren and Sid Unwin. In 1907 these women decided to take a side trip up the Alexandra and Castleguard river valleys on their way home from visiting Fortress Lake.

Their food supply was running low, so the men headed to a cache they had left downstream in one of Jimmy Simpson's winter cabins. The women were waiting in camp near the junction of the Alexandra and Saskatchewan rivers when who should appear but Jimmy Simpson himself. He undoubtedly would have approved of their planned trip up the Alexandra River; his experience trapping and guiding in the area had led him to declare it one of the most beautiful valleys in the Rockies.

Upon the men's return, the Schäffer party headed up the Alexandra, which they named Nashan-esen. The name, meaning "wolverine-go-quick," had been given to Simpson by the Stoneys in honour of his speed on snowshoes. Schäffer justified the change from "West-Branch-of-the-North-Fork-of-the-Saskatchewan," explaining that "Jim's axe in this country has done more to make the old trails passable for future comers than any others, and this little tribute to his labours seems small enough, – to name a beautiful valley and river for one who has helped to make a hard road easier."[5] Unfortunately the name was not officially adopted. In 1902 James Outram had already named an adjacent mountain and the river after Queen Alexandra, a favourite of the British public.

After reaching Watchman Creek, the Schäffer party turned west and climbed up to Watchman Lake, near the summit of Thompson Pass. Schäffer was very impressed with the lake, where "the horses were soon up to their necks in alpine flowers. Columbines nodded their yellow heads from stalks three feet [0.9 metres] tall, while deep blue larkspurs, snowy valerian, flaming castilleia, and golden arnicas hailed our coming with flying colours."[6]

There being no trail from the lake to the pass, the men went ahead on foot to seek out a route. The ascent to the pass was short and steep, requiring manoeuvring around a series of rock ledges. In Schäffer's words: "The ascent of the pass was full of those minor incidents which accompany the breaking of a new trail with horses, the steep, heavily wooded hill-slopes being interspersed with horizontally placed rock ridges, which were a trial to the flesh."[7]

Having successfully ascended the pass, the adventurers climbed a short distance up Mount Bryce to soak in the view of the Columbia Icefield. They returned to camp at Watchman Lake for three days, where:

> the ceiling of our banquet-hall was the blue sky of the Rockies, the walls the brave old hills themselves, and the orchestra a hermit-thrush singing his vesper notes ... health was good, hearts were light, and no ripple of worry from the outside world could touch us.... It was hard to go from that beautiful place, to leave the little lake to the butterflies, the gophers, the ducks, the bears, and the flowers. But neither our coming nor going left one ripple on her placid face; born to loneliness she would not miss us.[8]

They returned to the Saskatchewan for more exploring in the Front Ranges.

Opposite above: Packer Sid Unwin assisted Mary Schäffer and Mollie Adams on their trips.

Opposite below: The magnificent Alexandra valley, named Nashan-esen by Mary Schäffer.

SCIENTISTS

Twelve years after Schäffer's party explored Nashan-esen, a beehive of activity broke the silence in the Thompson Pass area: the Inter-provincial Boundary Survey, under the direction of A.O. Wheeler, had begun its work between Thompson Pass, the Castleguard Meadows, and Fortress Lake.

One of Wheeler's men, Swiss guide Conrad Kain, decided he would stay the winter, trapping with Jimmy Simpson along the Castleguard and Alexandra rivers. On the days the survey party could not work that summer, Kain established cabins and shelters along the lines he would trap. All seemed ready – except that Simpson turned out not to be able to make it, leaving Kain to stay on alone. In February 1920 Kain came out on foot along the North Saskatchewan. On a tree on the Mistaya River, he wrote on a blaze: "A hell of a trip-soft snow."[9]

The following year, Charles Walcott,[10] his wife Mary Vaux Walcott, camp manager and cook Arthur Brown, and packers Billy Lewis and Cecil Smith spent part of the summer in the Castleguard Meadows area. As they moved up the Saskatchewan toward the Alexandra on August 28, Walcott, who was constantly studying geology, noted in his diary: "Taking photographs A.M. of trails on river mud and of quartzite cliffs beneath Devonian on end of Mt. Wilson cliffs.... The valley is broad & flat at the point with broad anticlinal structure."[11]

They spent the night camped on the gravel flats of the West Branch of the North Fork (Alexandra River). In the morning, the Walcotts went on ahead of the pack train and found the trail leading up the Castleguard River. Several difficult fords left the entire party with damp feet. Walcott later explained that at the end of the gravel flats on the Castleguard:

> We came to a canyon and the trail was blazed in the woods.
> We soon began to go up and for an hour climbed through
> the brush, over logs and slippery turf. At last the forest began
> to thin out and soon we went up a steep slope and this large

A.O. Wheeler, co-founder of the Alpine Club of Canada, learned mountain climbing as part of his profession. Many of his geological surveys had to be taken from high on a mountaintop.

Alpine valley [Castleguard Meadows] was spread out before us. It is surrounded by high ridges and glaciers and a fine stream flows though it. Clumps of spruce trees occur and near one of these we found a relatively level spot. The rain ceased for a time and by dark tents were up and Arthur had a fine dinner. We later put up our camp stove in the tent and were dry and warm when turning in for the night.[12]

The weather remained cold, wet, and cloudy for the duration of their stay. On September 1, they visited a cave Cecil Smith had discovered a half-mile (0.8 kilometre) below camp while looking for the horses. It turned out to be the entrance to the Castleguard Cave, the longest known cave in Canada. With no end in sight to the dreary weather, they cancelled their planned visit to the Thompson Pass area, returned to the Saskatchewan River, and headed east toward the Kootenay Plains.

Opposite: Conrad Kain, highly regarded mountain climbing guide, often spent his winters trapping in remote parts of the Rocky Mountains.

Below: The Castleguard Meadows, looking north.

Over the Icefield

In 1923 Dr. J. Monroe Thorington and his friend Dr. William Ladd asked Jimmy Simpson to outfit an expedition to the region, the first mountaineers to do so in twenty-one years. With Simpson as guide, assisted by Ulysses La Casse and Tommy Frayne, the party left Lake Louise on June 27.[13] "We had quite an audience," Thorington explained, "… for the start of a pack-train is a thing not seen every day. Such a commotion! Boxes and saddles; duffle bags and pans. Squealing horses tethered in the scrub-pine, breaking loose now and then and galloping through the clearing, bells clanging and pack-covers flapping…. A heave and a buck; profanity and the operation repeated … off at last with the horses fighting for their place in line."[14]

On July 1, after six days on the trail, they turned up the Alexandra River and made camp near the Alexandra Glacier. The seventh day took them to Watchman Creek, which flows from Thompson Pass. Unable to resist its call, they set up camp on nearby gravel flats, then followed in Mary Schäffer's footsteps by tracing the creek to its source and proceeding to the pass. On July 5, they climbed over the steep shoulder of Terrace Mountain to the Castleguard Meadows, where everyone's attention turned to the peaks.

After nearly two weeks of climbing, they set their sights northward. Previously, those wishing to continue north from the area had been forced to spend three days retracing their steps down the Alexandra River to the Saskatchewan and over Sunwapta Pass. According to Thorington, "for many years there had existed, among the outfitters, the desire to find a direct route practicable for horses between the heads of the Castleguard and Sunwapta River."[15]

Simpson had explored the possibilities and concluded that a direct route across the glacier would be difficult but possible. He led the expedition across the Castleguard Meadows, onto the shore of a flat moraine, and right onto the Saskatchewan Glacier! Thorington explained that the horses, "at first timid, … soon became accustomed to their surroundings and, like true mountaineers, hopped over the little cracks and crevasses…. The horses were taken down the glacier for more than four miles [6.4 kilometres]…. The steep terminal moraine … was most troublesome, requiring some trail building and considerable care to avoid damage to the pack-train."[16]

The party proceeded over Parker Ridge to arrive at Sunwapta Pass on July 17, saving two days of travelling time. They then continued on to Bow Pass and Lake Louise. This was the first time a pack train had been taken across a glacier, and the feat won Simpson a great deal of respect in outfitting and guiding circles.

A mere two weeks after Thorington left the Castleguard Meadows, the Appalachian Mountaineering Club group arrived (see Route I on page 57), filling the valley with the sounds of adventure. They spent four days on the Meadows before using the newly minted Saskatchewan Glacier shortcut to Camp Parker and Wilcox Pass.

Jimmy Simpson with his pack train on the Saskatchewan Glacier. Simpson was the first outfitter to take his horses onto the ice.

The following year, members of a sister mountaineering club made their way to the Castleguard Meadows. W. Osgood Field; his brother, Fred; and their friend Lem Harris were members of the new Harvard Mountaineering Club. Their outfitter and guide was Max Brooks of Banff, who, along with packers Ernie Stanton and Cecil Smith, brought enough supplies for a month of camping and climbing. Swiss guides Edward Feuz and Joseph Biner rounded out the party.

The eager mountaineers spent five days travelling the Bow Summit route to the North Saskatchewan River. Another two long, hard days saw them journey up the Alexandra and Castleguard rivers to the Castleguard Meadows, where they discovered none other than James Outram and seven companions camped nearby.

The Field party left on July 16, using Jimmy Simpson's glacier route to exit the Meadows. They met up with another piece of mountain history at the Saskatchewan River, where a Caroline Hinman party of twenty-four was camped (see Route I on pages 58–60). The groups shared a meal that evening, then carried on their respective ways the next day. The Field party arrived at Lake Louise on July 30, having climbed several more peaks along the way.[17]

Meanwhile, Hinman's party, which had set out from the Yoho Valley (see Route II on page 131–132) and reached the Saskatchewan via Amiskwi and Howse passes (see Route I on page 58–60), proceeded toward the Alexandra River. They continued up the Alexandra and Castleguard rivers, setting up camp on the Castleguard Meadows on July 22. Staying in a beautiful spot for several days was a regular feature of Hinman's trips; her customers were able to enjoy the meadows until July 28.

During this time, Hinman's group rode to Thompson Pass, where the women left the men at the lower lake (Watchman) and proceeded for a swim in the upper lake (Cinema). Another day, they rode out onto the Saskatchewan Glacier.

They also climbed Castleguard Mountain and explored the mouth of the cave.[18] On July 28 they left the Castleguard Meadows to return to Lake Louise via Pinto Pass, the Cline River, Whiterabbit Pass, and the Cascade River.[19] Hinman enjoyed the area so much she returned the following year, accompanied by her friend Lillian Gest.

Above: An old trapper's cabin at Watchman Lake, similar to those Conrad Kain and other trappers would have used.

Left: Caroline Hinman led her Off the Beaten Track tours throughout the Canadian Rockies.

A month after the Hinman party left the Castleguard Meadows, two other outfits were making their way up the Alexandra River. Byron Harmon, Banff's famous mountain photographer, and his friend Lewis Freeman, a freelance writer and adventurer, left Lake Louise on August 16 on a seventy-day, five-hundred-mile (eight-hundred-kilometre) pack train trip to Jasper. Head guide was Soapy Smith, assisted by wrangler Rob Baptie and cook Ulysses La Casse. Sixteen horses and two dogs rounded out the party.

The adventurers proceeded over Bow Summit to the Alexandra River, camping a mile (1.6 kilometres) below the Alexandra Glacier on the evening of August 28. That night another outfit arrived, led by Soapy Smith's partner, Bill Potts. He was escorting a Dr. Fowler and his son from New York and Dr. Atkins of Banff.[20]

The two parties travelled together down the Castleguard River to the Meadows. Freeman had brought a radio and was anxious to see if radio reception was possible in the remote mountains. After considerable effort, the radio began receiving clear signals. For the remaining two months of the expedition, the world came to visit every night. (Today many groups go into the mountains without radios to avoid having the world come to visit every night!)

After a week of photography and mountain climbing from their base in the Castleguard Meadows, the Freeman/Harmon party prepared to proceed along Jimmy Simpson's Saskatchewan Glacier route. On the morning of September 6, each man led a group of three to four horses tied head to tail onto the ice. Getting off the ice proved somewhat more complicated. The horses had to slide down a narrow ramp of ice flanked by deep crevasses on either side. Daunting as the feat was, all went smoothly, including Harmon's photography of the event.[21] The party continued over Wilcox Pass to the Athabasca River and continued on to Jasper, with several side trips to such photogenic spots as the base of Mount Columbia and Fortress Lake.

Opposite above: Byron Harmon travelled widely in the Canadian Rockies as part of his efforts to photograph all the major peaks.

Opposite below: Lewis Freeman and his radio. Freeman was anxious to bring the world to visit every night while in the backcountry.

Above: Leopold Amery (r) politician, world traveller, and mountaineer with his friend A.O. Wheeler, co-founder of the Alpine Club of Canada.

Right: Cliff and Ruth Kopas just before their marriage in Calgary in 1933. They left shortly thereafter to travel overland by horseback to the Pacific.

The End of an Era

In 1929 the Alexandra valley bore witness to a man on a mission. Leopold Charles Morris Stennett Amery was a British politician, world traveller, and mountaineer. A quiet, modest man, he was courteous and kind to all who came near him, be they royalty or a simple packer on the trail. Amery had always wanted to traverse the country between Lake Louise and Jasper and, in particular, to visit the Columbia Icefield. But, he explained:

> I also had a particular motive – of vanity, perhaps – for se-
> lecting that route for this occasion. Two years before, the
> Geographical Board of Canada had done me the hon-
> our of naming after me a mountain at the junction of the
> Alexandra and Saskatchewan Rivers.... [Mountains are] of-
> ten ... called after more or less eminent elderly gentlemen
> who have never seen them, let alone thought of ascending
> them. To me the challenge was obvious. Why not make sure,
> as there was apparently still time to do, of raising Mt. Amery
> in the Rockies from the latter to the former category, and of
> proving myself, as a mountaineer and not merely as a politi-
> cian, justified of the appellation? [22]

Amery, now approaching sixty, arrived in Banff on August 13, 1929, accompanied by the CPR's Brian Meredith. Meredith, a publicity man, had arranged for the Brewsters to provide an outfit and hired Edward Feuz as climbing guide. Amery's friend A.O. Wheeler was also to accompany them on the first leg of the journey.

The party left Lake Louise on August 15, proceeding north to the mouth of the Alexandra River. They set up camp three miles [4.8 kilometres] upriver, a convenient place from which to attempt Mount Amery. In spite of inclement weather, Amery, Feuz, and Meredith succeeded in ascending the peak the following day. Back in camp, "there turned up that splendid trail-riding guide, Jimmy Simpson, with his 'dudes,' i.e., tourists, in the shape of five pretty and jolly American college girls whom he had taken up to see the Columbia Icefield."[23]

On August 22 the party moved on to the Castleguard Meadows for more climbing. Three days later, Wheeler, Meredith, and one of the wranglers left for Lake Louise; on September 1 the remainder of the party left for the Saskatchewan. None suspected the devastating economic collapse which was to severely curtail journeys such as theirs.

Neither, unfortunately, did Jack Brewster, who set up his Jasper to Lake Louise "Glacier Trail" expeditions in the late 1920s. He took clients from Jasper to Maligne Lake, then over Jonas and Nigel passes to the Saskatchewan. They followed the trail up the Alexandra River to the Castleguard Meadows, returned to the Saskatchewan by the same route, then proceeded over Bow Summit and on to Lake Louise. The Brewsters had set up a string of camps along the route to accommodate visitors, but their timing was just not right. The venture was devastated by the Depression. Leonard Leacock,[24] who spent a summer working at one of the Castleguard Meadows camps during this period, reported that only one party ever got as far as his camp.[25]

A most unusual procession did, however, make its way through the Castleguard Meadows in the summer of 1933. In the height of the Depression, Cliff Kopas and his new bride, Ruth, had decided to head from southern Alberta west to the Pacific.

Between them, they owned five horses and had $2.65 in cash. They set off for the Kananaskis Lakes in June, then wound their way through the Rockies, past Mount Assiniboine, and on to the Sunshine Meadows and the Bow River. They stopped at Bow Lake to visit with Jimmy Simpson before camping in the Castleguard Meadows. From there they headed east to Brazeau Lake and back over Poboktan Pass to the Sunwapta. They followed the Sunwapta and Athabasca rivers to Jasper, visited the Tonquin Valley, then headed west over Yellowhead Pass. After four months' travel, the young couple reached Bella Coola. Though Cliff remained in Bella Coola, he and Keith managed to develop a strong bond.[26]

Unfortunately the story does not have a happy ending. The following spring the young couple were able to take a motorboat trip to Mackenzie Rock, thus completing their amazing odyssey. However, only sixteen months after arriving in Bella Coola, Ruth died of complications during childbirth. Their son, Keith, was adopted by Ruth's sister and husband in Calgary. Still, over the years, Cliff and Keith were able to develop a strong bond. Cliff died in Bella Coola in 1978.

The Trail Today

The historic route along the Alexandra and Castleguard rivers to the Castleguard Meadows is a rugged hike that will appeal to those seeking solitude amidst beautiful scenery. Because the trail to the Castleguard Meadows is no longer maintained by Parks Canada, it requires some route-finding skills and has many unbridged stream crossings, depending on the time of year.

Except for the Castleguard Meadows themselves, this is a random camping area. On the Meadows, you must camp in a Special Preservation Zone, with camping allowed only within one hundred metres of the sign (see trail guide on page 181). Finding a camping spot along other parts of the route should not present a problem. The old campgrounds have been indicated in the trail guide and you are never far from water or large trees for food storage.

There is very little elevation gain between the trailhead and Outram's Shower Bath Falls,[27] whose outflow runs along the edge of the gravel flats perpendicular to the trail leading to Thompson Pass.

But while most of the route's stream crossings are quite easy, the outlet from the Shower Bath Falls is the most difficult crossing I have attempted in more than 3,200 kilometres of hiking throughout the Rockies. A trail marked with blue flagging tape appears to offer an alternative to the difficult ford, but it in fact turns to the right and climbs the mountainside to view the subterranean source of the waterfalls. It is worth a side trip to see the phenomenon of waterfalls emerging directly from the side of the mountain, but the trail does not allow you to circumvent the difficult crossing.

As I entered the stream, it was very cold, very deep, and very fast flowing. Its force tore my river-crossing sandals from my feet, leaving the shoes to dangle from my ankles as I crossed. The current was so strong I could not lift my feet; fortunately the pain of dragging them along the rocks was numbed by the frigid water. My saving grace was the metal ski pole I carry for river crossings. It provided stability as I shuffled along, two to three centimetres at a time, never moving more than one foot or

Tongue of the Saskatchewan Glacier in 2005.
The receding glacier would have been much
farther east when Simpson first took his pack
train across in 1923.

175

the pole at a time. A wooden pole would not have worked; it would have floated and likely been torn from my hands.

As I progressed, the stream kept getting deeper. More than once, I wondered if I should keep going, as I was alone and it was unlikely there was anyone else within thirty kilometres. I did continue and made it safely across, but the prospect of having to repeat the performance was not appealing. On my return, I camped by the base of the falls to enable an early-morning crossing. The slightly decreased flow made the crossing marginally easier. (Glacier-fed streams tend to decrease their flow during the cool night, as melting of the glacier decreases during that time.) The ford would likely be much easier in late September, or during a cool spell, which would decrease the quantity of glacial melt. It is possible the current warming trend in the mountains has increased the flow, as no other guide book mentions this as a difficult crossing.

From the far side of the outlet, it is a short, steep climb to the Castleguard Meadows. The gravel flats of the Alexandra and Castleguard rivers offer good views and some spectacular scenery. The trail is generally easy to follow, though some route-finding skills are required in sections that may be flooded or washed out on the gravel flats.

The Castleguard Meadows are beautiful, and most hikers could happily spend a few days exploring the area. Exiting the Meadows normally requires returning by the same route. On the return, a side trip to Thompson Pass is well worth the effort. The main challenge here is fording the Castleguard River. But because it is highly braided on these gravel flats, it should be relatively easy to cross on shallow streams between gravel bars. Once across the river, a short uphill climb leads to two beautiful lakes and on to the pass. An abandoned cabin – probably an old trapper's cabin – near the end of Watchman Lake reminds hikers of the region's history.

The walk across the meadow to the overlook of the Saskatchewan Glacier is easy and well worth the trip. However, hikers should not attempt to go out onto the ice unless they are experienced in glacier travel and have brought the necessary equipment.

Remains of a corduroy road left by the United States Army. During the Second World War, the Saskatchewan Glacier was used to test vehicles destined for use in the construction of the Alaska Highway.

For those who do not have the skills and/or equipment for glacier travel, the tongue of the receding Saskatchewan Glacier can be viewed after an easy traverse from the Icefields Parkway, mainly across the gravel flats of the North Saskatchewan River. The hike to the tongue is on an old road the United States army built during the Second World War to enable them to test equipment on the glacier.

The scenery from the gravel flats is often dramatic, but it pales in comparison with the route's end. The hike terminates at a small lake backed by a sheer wall of thick, dramatically blue ice. Off to the left and high above hide the Castleguard Meadows, which are not discernible from this viewpoint.

Trail Guide

Distances are adapted from existing trail guides: Patton and Robinson, Potter, and Beers, and from Gem-Trek maps. Distances intermediate from those given in the sources are estimated from topographical maps and from hiking times. All distances are in kilometres.

From the North Saskatchewan River to the Castleguard Meadows

Maps   83 C/2 Cline River
            83 C/3 Columbia Icefield
            Bow Lake and Saskatchewan Crossing (Gem Trek)

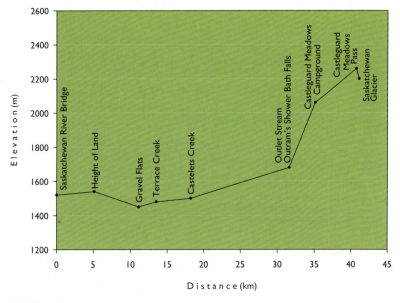

Trailhead

The beginning of the trail is not obvious from the road. Follow the Icefields Parkway (Hwy. 93) 26 km north from the junction with Highway 11 or 9.5 km north from the Sunset Pass trailhead (this signboard is not marked from the parkway). If you reach the Cirrus Mountain Campground, you have gone 2 km too far. There is a widening of the roadway at the trailhead and this pullout acts as a parking area for the trail. From the north end of the parking area, the trail heads downhill on an old road.

0.0	Bridge across the North Saskatchewan River. The trail is an old road that parallels the Icefields Parkway.
1.3	Cross a rapidly flowing creek on a log bridge. Continue through the trees in a narrow valley.
1.9	Cross an avalanche path that affords good views of the mountains on both sides.
3.9	Gravel flats of the North Saskatchewan River.
5.1	Cross a height of land as the old road curves to the west toward the Alexandra valley. Drop steadily toward the river with occasional views through the trees.
10.4	Calf-deep ford of an unbridged stream.
11.1	Enter the gravel flats. The river is broad and shallow here. It is preferable to travel on the gravel flats if possible. During periods of high water, hikers may wish to use the trail (of sorts) along the bank.
11.7	The old road on the gravel flats enters the forest and follows the river, staying in the trees.
13.5	Knee-high ford of fast-flowing Terrace Creek. There is a campground across the creek from the old bridge site. Downstream, the road once forded the creek. This is a good ford. Farther downstream is the site of an old cabin, outbuildings, and a corral. Part of the cabin is still standing. After the campground, the trail soon rejoins the gravel flats, goes inland to cross a headland, then makes its way back to the scenic flats.
18.2	Mid-calf ford of Castelets Creek. Only the footings of the old bridge remain. Soon re-enter the gravel flats and continue up the valley. Toward the end of the gravel flats, the road curves

northwest toward an obvious break in the mountains: the Castleguard valley.

20.7   End of the gravel flats. There is a white painted sign here pointing toward the single-track trail and indicating that the Castleguard Meadows are 8 miles (12.9 km) away. The trail climbs a small ridge.

21.4   Castleguard River Warden Cabin. There is an old campsite on the right (north) a short distance ahead. The trail continues through the forest, often rooty and wet.

23.5   Cross a creek on a fallen log. Follow along the narrow, fast-flowing river with rapids and waterfalls.

29.8   Knee-deep ford across a fast-flowing rocky stream – care required. The trail continues along the river bank.

31.6   Come to a rapidly flowing stream with a trail leading uphill marked by blue flagging tape. Do not follow the tape unless you wish to take a side trip to view the source of Outram's Shower Bath Falls. When the trail starts uphill, turn left (west) onto the river flats, cross a small stream, and proceed to the outlet stream from the falls. When I was there in the middle of July, this stream was crotch-deep, fast, cold, and rocky, making the crossing treacherous, even with the assistance of a metal hiking pole. (Other guide books either do not mention this ford or only make passing mention of it. This may mean that later in the year, the ford is easier.) After fording the stream, continue upstream on the gravel flats past two small waterfalls to the base of the main fall.

31.9   On the edge of the gravel flats just beyond the fall, there is an old painted sign on a fallen tree that reads "Castleguard Meadows, 1 mi [1.6 km]." There is a campsite here. Large blazes on the trees mark the beginning of the trail, which climbs fairly steeply up the side of the mountain. Near the top are fabulous views to the left (west), including some of Thompson Pass. The trail soon levels off on a plateau of open meadows and some forest.

Head east and slightly north on a faint trail, which heads toward a major stream. Across the stream, near a small waterfall, is a blank white sign in a tree.

35.1   Ford the stream above the waterfall (easy ford) to the campground marked by the sign. To go to the end of the meadow and view the Saskatchewan Glacier, cross the stream to the west side and head north on the open meadow. There is no trail.

37.0   End of the relatively flat portion of the meadow; start climbing the first ridge.

38.1   Top of the first ridge. Continue on through the meadow; glacier is visible on the left (west).

40.7   Top of the pass. Start to lose altitude; cross another ridge.

41.1   The tongue of the Saskatchewan Glacier is spread out below. This is the end of the Meadows. Do not proceed onto the glacier unless you are trained in glacier travel and have the proper equipment.

Proceeding north along the Castleguard Meadows toward the tongue of the Saskatchewan Glacier, hikers are tantalized by glimpses of the Castleguard Glaciers (left).

From the Castleguard River to Thompson Pass

Map   83 C/3 Columbia Icefield

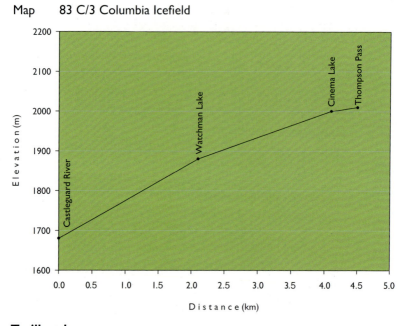

Trailhead

From the west side of the outflow from Outram's Shower Bath Falls, ford the Castleguard River by carefully choosing the easiest of the braided channels. The ford is generally not much more than knee deep. Follow the river a short distance downstream to approximately west of the twin falls; there is a white painted sign in a tree indicating the start of the Thompson Pass hike.

0.0   Painted sign in a tree, west of the Castleguard River. The trail initially leads steeply uphill through dense forest to the top of a ridge, then climbs gently.

1.1   Major stream on the left (south) is the outflow from Watchman Lake. The trail skirts the edge of a marshy area and passes a small waterfall.

2.1   Northeast end of Watchman Lake. About halfway along the lake there is an old outfitter's camp. At the end of the lake is a very old sign in a tree marking a camping spot, which was complete with a pile of split firewood in 2003. The trail around the end of the lake is obscure; from the end of the lake it heads uphill through forest.

3.7   Top of the ridge. The trail continues on a downhill slope and crosses a series of small meadows.

4.1   Cinema Lake. The trail goes around the lake, crosses a small meadow, and climbs over a small rocky ridge.

4.5   Thompson Pass and the National Park boundary. Straight ahead is a large, swampy meadow.

Cinema Lake, where Caroline Hinman and her female companions enjoyed swimming and bathing after leaving the men behind at Watchman Lake. Situated very close to the Continental Divide near Thompson Pass, Cinema Lake was named for the reflective properties of its water.

From the Big Bend in the Icefields Parkway to the Saskatchewan Glacier

Map   83 C/3 Columbia Icefield

The elevation gradually increases by 200 m over the 7.2-km distance.

Trailhead

Take the Icefields Parkway to the Big Bend of the highway, approximately 11 km south of the Banff/Jasper Park boundary. If you are travelling north, there is a break in the guard rail on the left, partway down toward the hairpin curve on the open gravel flats. At the break, turn left onto an old road leading to a bridge. There is parking for a small number of cars before the bridge. If you miss the turn, proceed to the pullout on the gravel flats, turn around, and return. The old road and bridge are obvious when heading south.

0.0   Trailhead. Cross the concrete bridge, continue on the old road for 15 m, then turn right on a footpath that goes to the top of the bank and joins up with an old US Army road.

0.8   Remnants of an old bridge or corduroy road as the road heads out onto the gravel flats. Cross the gravel flats, following the piles of stone.

1.2   Enter the woods at the end of the gravel flats, climb over a small ridge, and drop back down to the gravel flats.

2.6   Entrance to gravel flats. There is a small log structure here with a dramatic view across the gravel flats to Mount Saskatchewan and the glacier in the background.

3.9   Begin a long stretch where the road is washed out. An obvious trail follows the top of the riverbank. It is best to stay on the gravel flats as long as possible; the riverbank trail eventually returns to the old road.

4.5   Old road enters the gravel flats and continues, marked by rock piles. Eventually, it becomes a trail.

6.2   A good trail passes a pile of stones with a wooden cross, which is a Water Resources Branch marker. As the trail gets closer to the lake at the tongue of the glacier, it is marked by stone cairns.

7.2   End of the trail at the lakeshore. The glacier is a sheer wall of ice. Hikers should only attempt to go onto the ice if they are experienced in glacier travel and are properly equipped.

The Saskatchewan Glacier, seen from the northern end of the Castleguard Meadows. This is close to the spot where Simpson would have led his pack train onto the ice, although glacial melt over the past century has drastically changed its appearance since then.

NOTES

INTRODUCTION

1. Tom Wilson, "Memories of Golden Days," *Canadian Alpine Journal* 14 (1924): 124–25.

2. J. Monroe Thorington, *The Glittering Mountains of Canada* (Philadelphia: John W. Lea, 1925), 9.

ROUTE I

1. Jon Whyte, *Indians in the Rockies* (Canmore: Altitude, 1985), 24.

2. For a brief biographical sketch of David Thompson, see Emerson Sanford and Janice Sanford Beck, *Life of the Trail 1* (Calgary: Rocky Mountain Books, 2008), 24-27.

3. Quoted in Arthur S. Morton, *A History of the Canadian West to 1870-71*, 2nd ed., ed. Lewis G. Thomas (Toronto: University of Toronto Press, 1973), 481.

4. See *Life of the Trail 1*, 24–29, for more details of this trip.

5. Jack Nisbet, *Sources of the River: Tracking David Thompson across Western North America* (Seattle: Sasquatch Books, 1994), 68.

6. Ibid., 72.

7. The Tobacco Plains is an area east of the Kootenay River on the present Canada/US border. As the Tobacco Plains Kootenai use the American spelling (Kootenai), it is used in this section. The remainder of this book uses the Canadian spelling, Kootenay.

8. Nisbet, 73–74.

9. Nisbet, 84.

10. See *Life of the Trail 1*, 91–93, for more information about the Kootenay Plains.

11. D'Arcy Jenish, *Epic Wanderer: David Thompson and the Mapping of the Canadian West.* (Toronto: Doubleday Canada, 2003), 128.

12. Nisbet, 88.

13. Joyce and Peter McCart, *On the Road with David Thompson* (Calgary: Fifth House, 2000), 141-42.

14. Morton, 496.

15. Anne (McMullen) Belliveau, *Small Moments in Time: The Story of Alberta's Big West Country* (Calgary: Detselig Enterprises, 1999), 61.

16. See *Life of the Trail 1*, 72–79, for more information about Hector's travels.

17. See above.

18. Bruce Haig, *Following Historic Trails: James Hector, Explorer* (Calgary: Detselig Enterprises, 1983), 28–31.

19. For a description of this trip see *Life of the Trail 1*, 73.

20. John Palliser, *The Papers of the Palliser Expedition, 1857-1860*, ed. Irene M. Spry (Toronto: The Champlain Society, 1968), 446.

21. Daphne Sleigh, *Walter Moberly and the Northwest Passage by Rail* (Surrey, BC: Hancock House Publishers, 2003), 66–67.

22. Pierre Berton, *The National Dream: The Great Railway, 1871-1881* (Toronto: McClelland & Stewart, 1970), 165–67.

23. See R.M. Rylatt for a detailed account of life on the Blaeberry River during the winter of 1871–72.

24. Sleigh, 178–81.

25. Ibid., 180.

26. Thomas E. Wilson, *Trailblazer of the Canadian Rockies* (Calgary: Glenbow-Alberta Institute, 1972), 33.

27. Walter D. Wilcox, "Bill Peyto," in *Tales from the Canadian Rockies*, ed. Brian Patton (Edmonton: Hurtig, 1984), 151.

28. Ibid.

29. H.E.M. Stutfield and J. Norman Collie, *Climbs and Explorations in the Canadian Rockies* (Calgary: Aquila Books, 1998), 59-60.

30. Ibid., 61.

31. Ibid., 63.

32. Ian Allison Ludlow Getty, *A Historical Guide to Yoho National Park* (Ottawa: Department of Indian Affairs and Northern Development, 1972), 13.

33. Stutfield and Collie, 63.

34. There does not appear to be a record of when and why the name was changed from Baker Pass to Amiskwi Pass. We have used the name Baker when the travellers themselves did so; otherwise we use the current name, Amiskwi.

35. For more information about the Pipestone Pass trail, see *Life of the Trail 1*, 73–112.

36. E.J. Hart, *Ain't it Hell: Bill Peyto's "Mountain Journal"* (Banff: EJH Literary Enterprises, 1995), 59–62.

37. James Outram, *In the Heart of the Canadian Rockies* (New York: Macmillan, 1905), 213.

38. Elizabeth Parker, "In Memoriam: Edward Whymper," *Canadian Alpine Journal* 4 (1912): 133.

39. Mrs. Charles Schäffer, *Untrodden Paths in the Canadian Rockies* (Minneapolis: Powers Mercantile Company, n.d).

40. J.E.C. Eaton, "An Expedition to the Freshfield Group," *Canadian Alpine Journal* 3 (1911): 1.

41. For a brief biography of J.W.A. Hickson, see *Life of the Trail 1*, 37-39.

42. J.W.A. Hickson, "A Visit to the Saskatchewan Valley and Mount Forbes," *Canadian Alpine Journal* 12 (1922): 26.

43. J. Monroe Thorington, *The Glittering Mountains of Canada* (Philadelphia: John W. Lea, 1925), 17.

44. J. Monroe Thorington, "The Freshfield Group, 1922" *Canadian Alpine Journal* 13 (1923): 69.

45. Esther Fraser, *Wheeler* (Banff: Summerthought, 1978), 114.

46. F.N. Waterman, "From Field to Mount Robson – Summer 1923" *Canadian Alpine Journal* 14 (1924): 114.

47. Ellis L. Yochelson, *Smithsonian Institution Secretary, Charles Doolittle Walcott* (Kent, Ohio: Kent State University Press, 2001), 271–72.

48. For more information on Hinman's trips, see *Life of the Trail 1*, 54–56.

49. Lillian Gest fonds, Whyte Museum of the Canadian Rockies, M67/41, 18.

50. Ibid., 18–19.

51. Ibid., 21.

52. For directions from Golden to the turnoff to the Ensign Creek logging road, see Patton and Robinson, 311; and Beers, 160.

Route II

1. Carson Wade, *Human History of Yoho National Park* (Parks Canada, 1978), 3.

2. Quoted in R.W. Sandford, *Yoho: A History and Celebration of Yoho National Park* (Canmore: Altitude, 1993), 45.

3. Wade, 29.

4. Quoted in Don Beers, *The Wonder of Yoho: Scenes, Tales, Trails* (Calgary: Rocky Mountain Books, 1989), 142.

5. Quoted in James Simpson, "Days Remembered," *American Alpine Journal* 19 (1974): 49.

6. Jean Habel, "The North Fork of the Wapta," *Appalachia* 8 (1896–98): 328.

7. Ralph Edwards, *The Trail to the Charmed Land* (Victoria: Herbert R. Larson, 1950), 17.

8. Habel, 330.

9. Edwards, 28.

10. Quoted in Beers, 177.

11. Edwards, 12.

12. Quoted in Beers, 134.

13. Janice Sanford Beck, *No Ordinary Woman: The Story of Mary Schäffer Warren* (Calgary: Rocky Mountain Books, 2001), 21.

14. Susan Warrender, *"Mr. Banff": The Story of Norman Luxton* (Calgary: Alistair Bear Enterprises, 2003), 20.

15. Robert William Sandford, *Emerald Lake Lodge: A History and Celebration* (Field: Canadian Rocky Mountain Resorts, 2002), 24–25.

16. George F.G. Stanley, "John Hammond: Painter for the CPR," *The CPR West: The Iron Road and the Making of a Nation*, ed. Hugh A. Dempsey (Vancouver: Douglas & McIntyre, 1984), 213–15.

17. *Saint John Daily Sun*, "Prof. Hammond, Director of Mount Allison Art Department, Tells of His Visit to the Rockies," n.d., 1901, in Hammond Papers, Owens Art Gallery, Mount Allison University, Sackville, NB.

18. Ibid.

19. Beers, 88.

20. Quoted. in Beers, 93.

21. Hammond Papers.

22. George S. Vaux, Jr., "The Wapta Fall," *Appalachia* 9 (1899–1901): 314.

23. Cyndi Smith fonds, Whyte Museum of the Canadian Rockies, M158.

24. James Outram, *In the Heart of the Canadian Rockies* (New York: Macmillan, 1906), 190.

25. Beryl Hallworth and Monica Jackson, *Pioneer Naturalists of the Rocky Mountains and the Selkirks* (Calgary: Calgary Field Naturalists Society, 1985), 4.

26. "Canada's First Alpine Club Camp," *Canadian Alpine Journal* 1:1 (1907): 56.

27. Julia W. Henshaw, "The Mountain Wildflowers of Western Canada," *Canadian Alpine Journal* 1:1 (1907): 133.

28. "Canada's First Alpine Club Camp," 51.

29. Brian Brennan, *Romancing the Rockies: Mountaineers, Missionaries, Marilyn and More* (Calgary: Fifth House, 2005), 82.

30. Quoted in Cyndi Smith, *Off the Beaten Track: Women Adventurers and Mountaineers in Western Canada* (Lake Louise: Coyote Books, 1989), 70.

31. Ibid.

32. Quoted in Sanford Beck, 64.

33. E.J. Hart, *Jimmy Simpson: Legend of the Rockies* (Canmore: Altitude, 1993), 46.

34. Godfrey A. Solly, "A Fortnight with the Canadian Alpine Club," *Canadian Alpine Journal* 2 (1910): 138.

35. Ellis L. Yochelson, *Smithsonian Institution Secretary, Charles Doolittle Walcott* (Ohio: Kent State University Press, 2001), 49.

36. Ibid.

37. Ibid.

38. Ibid., 66.

39. Ibid., 25, 47.

40. Ibid., 219.

41. Robert J. Burns with Mike Schintz, *Guardians of the Wild: A History of the Warden Service of Canada's National Parks* (Calgary: University of Calgary Press, 2000), 41–42.

42. Ibid., 31-33.

43. Bruce Hugh Russell, "J. Singer Sergeant in the Canadian Rockies," *The Beaver* 77:6 (Dec.1997–Jan.1998): 4.

44. Ibid.

45. Lisa Christensen, *A Hiker's Guide to Art of the Canadian Rockies* (Calgary: Glenbow-Alberta Institute, 1996), 89.

46. Lillian Gest fonds, Whyte Museum of the Canadian Rockies, M67/41, 17.

47. Gerry Adams, "Beyond the Rugged Mountains," *Alberta History* 36:1 (1988), 11.

48. Gary Bret Kines, *Chief Man-of-Many-Sides: John Murray Gibbon and his Contributions to the Development of Tourism and the Arts in Canada* (Ottawa: Carlton University, 2000), 57.

49. "General Rides and Central Pow-Wow," *Trail Riders of the Canadian Rockies Bulletin* 1 (Oct. 15, 1924): 1.

50. Hélène Déziel-Letnick with E.J. Hart, *At Rest in the Peaks A guided walk through the Old Banff Cemetery* (Banff: Whyte Museum of the Canadian Rockies, n.d.), 8–9.

51. Yochelson, 406.

52. Ibid., 463.

ROUTE III

1. It is possible that Aboriginal peoples, trappers, timber cullers, or other explorers had previously travelled through the area, but no such visits have been recorded.

2. James Outram, *In the Heart of the Canadian Rockies* (New York: Macmillan, 1906), 271.

3. Esther Fraser, *The Canadian Rockies: Early Travels and Explorations* (Edmonton:Hurtig, 1969), 176.

4. For a recent biography of Mary Schäffer Warren see Janice Sanford Beck, *No Ordinary Woman: The Story of Mary Schäffer Warren* (Calgary: Rocky Mountain Books, 2001).

5. Mary T.S. Schäffer, "Old Indian Trails: Expedition of 1907," *A Hunter of Peace*, ed. E.J. Hart (Banff: Whyte Museum of the Canadian Rockies, 1980), 51.

6. Ibid., 54.

7. Ibid., 53.

8. Ibid., 56.

9. Conrad Kain, *Where the Clouds Can Go* (New York: The American Alpine Club, 3rd ed., 1939), 379.

10. See Route II on pages 118–126 for details of the Walcotts' discovery of the Burgess Shale fossils.

11. Ellis L. Yochelson, *Smithsonian Institution Secretary, Charles Doolittle Walcott* (Ohio: Kent State University Press, 2001), 321.

12. Ibid., 322.

13. William Shadd and J. Monroe Thorington, "A Mountaineering Journey to the Columbia Icefield," *Canadian Alpine Journal* 14 (1924): 35.

14. J. Monroe Thorington, *The Glittering Mountains of Canada* (Philadelphia: John W. Lea, 1925), 56.

15. E.J. Hart, *Jimmy Simpson: Legend of the Rockies* (Canmore: Altitude, 1993), 140.

16. Thorington, 97.

17. W. Osgood Field, "Mountaineering on the Columbia Icefield" *Appalachia* 16 (1924–26): 144.

18. Lillian Gest fonds, 27–28.

19. For more details on this trip, see *Life of the Trail 1*, 167.

20. Lewis R. Freeman, *On the Roof of the Rockies* (Toronto: McClelland & Stewart, 1925), 13.

21. Peter and Catharine Whyte Foundation, ed. *Great Days in the Rockies: The Photographs of Byron Harmon 1906-1934* (Banff: Altitude, 1984), 19.

22. L.C.M.S. Amery, *In the Rain and the Sun* (New York: Hutchinson, 1946), 165.

23. Ibid., 168.

24. For a brief biographical sketch of Leonard Leacock, see *Life of the Trail 1, 147-148*.

25. Don Beers, *Banff-Assiniboine: A Beautiful World Scenes, Tales, Trails* (Calgary: Highline, 1993), 206.

26. Cliff Kopas, *Packhorses to the Pacific A Wilderness Honeymoon* (Victoria: Touch Wood Editions, 2004), 35-69.

27. The origin of the name for the falls is unknown, but Outram does comment on them in *In the Heart of the Canadian Rockies*. There is no indication that the falls provided him with anything other than a scenic backdrop.

IMAGE CREDITS

Page 20 In 1957 the Canadian government honoured David Thompson, Canada's great surveyor and map maker, by having his image depicted on a postage stamp. (Glenbow Museum and Archives, NA 1456-1.)

Page 39 Walter Moberly, seventh from the left, in a party of CPR surveyors. Moberly was convinced that Howse Pass was the best route for the railway. (Whyte Museum of the Canadian Rockies, V622/PA 128-18)

Page 41 Major A.B. Rogers, the irascible, tobacco-spitting, foul talking engineer-in-charge of the mountain section for the CPR, was nicknamed Hell's Bells Rogers. He was responsible for discovering Rogers Pass. (Glenbow Museum and Archives, NA 1949-1)

Page 43 Tom Wilson started his long life in the mountains as a packer and assistant to Major A.B. Rogers. He was the first non-Native to view both Lake Louise and Emerald Lake. (Whyte Museum of the Canadian Rockies, detail from V701/LC-90)

Page 45 Peter Sarbach standing, George Baker (l), and J. Norman Collie relaxing before a trip. These mountaineers were the first group to attempt the route over Amiskwi Pass. (Whyte Museum of the Canadian Rockies, V701/LC-9)

Page 47 Bill Peyto, a colourful, conscientious and highly respected guide, helped pioneer the route over Amiskwi Pass. (Whyte Museum of the Canadian Rockies, V683/NG-8-105)

Page 55 J. Monroe Thorington (centre) in camp with Swiss guide Edward Feuz, Jr. (l) and mountaineer Howard Palmer. (Whyte Museum of the Canadian Rockies, V622/PA128-17)

Page 55 Famous mountain guide Jimmy Simpson, leading a pack train. Simpson is perhaps best known for building Num Ti Jah Lodge on the shores of Bow Lake. (Whyte Museum of the Canadian Rockies, NA66-499)

Page 59 The Natural Bridge on the Kicking Horse River as it appeared early in the twentieth century. (Whyte Museum of the Canadian Rockies, V653/NA-80-912)

Page 80 Tom Wilson's stray horses led him to Emerald Lake, where the animals had likely been earlier with their Aboriginal owners. (Whyte Museum of the Canadian Rockies, detail from V701/LC-16)

Page 87 J.J. McArthur, the surveyor who first climbed Burgess Pass. A lake, a pass, and a creek in Yoho National Park are named after him. (National Archives of Canada, PA-42178)

Page 89 Professor Jean Habel, a loner who explored extensively in the Yoho Valley and near the headwaters of the Athabasca River. (Whyte Museum of the Canadian Rockies, V14/AC-175 P/1)

Page 93 The spectacular Yoho Glacier Cave, as Habel and his party would have seen it. (Whyte Museum of the Canadian Rockies, V653/NA80-525)

Page 95 (l–r) Unknown, Samuel Allen, C.S. Thompson, H.P. Nichols, and unknown. Allen walked along the Emerald River to become the second recorded non-Aboriginal person to see Emerald Lake. (Whyte Museum of the Canadian Rockies, detail from NA66-2143)

Page 96 Emerald Lake Cabins, shortly after completion, circa 1906. (Whyte Museum of the Canadian Rockies, V653/NG-4-726)

Page 99 John Hammond, artist, teacher, world traveller, and mountain explorer, took advantage of the CPR's offer of free transportation in exchange for art. (Mount Allison University Archives, 8800/3/2)

Page 103 Edward Whymper gained world fame as the first person to climb the Matterhorn. His work in the Canadian Rockies provided publicity for the CPR. (Whyte Museum of the Canadian Rockies, V14/AC 00P-251)

Page 110 Winnipeg journalist Elizabeth Parker was a key driving force in the founding of the Alpine Club of Canada (ACC). The very popular ACC hut at Lake O'Hara is named in her honour. (Whyte Museum of the Canadian Rockies, CAJ 1938 p. 92)

Page 113 Outfitter packing supplies and equipment from Field to Emerald Lake and over Yoho Pass into the ACC camp at Yoho Lake.(Whyte Museum of the Canadian Rockies, NA66-528)

Page 114 The 1906 ACC camp at Summit (Yoho) Lake. This was the club's first annual camp. A large number of tents were required to shelter the camp's 112 participants. Somehow the environment survived. (Whyte Museum of the Canadian Rockies, V653/NA80-487).

Page 117 (l–r) CPR publicist John Murray Gibbon with palaeontologist Charles Walcott and outfitter Tom Wilson. (Whyte Museum of the Canadian Rockies, C701/LC-98)

Page 119 The Yoho Valley Road as it appeared early in the twentieth century. (Whyte Museum of the Canadian Rockies, V263/NA71-2826).

Page 121 Dr. Charles Doolittle Walcott, the man who brought the Burgess Shale fossils to the world's attention. He mined huge quantities of fossil-bearing shale and shipped it to the Smithsonian Institute in Washington, DC. (Whyte Museum of the Canadian Rockies, V14/AC 00P-811)

Page 124 Helen Breese Walcott, daughter of Charles and Helene Walcott, wrote that it was her mother who actually discovered the first Burgess Shale fossil beds. (Whyte Museum of the Canadian Rockies, V263/NA71-562)

Page 128 Mary Vaux Walcott, the first woman to visit the Yoho Valley, spent most summers of her adult life in the Canadian Rockies. (Whyte Museum of the Canadian Rockies, AAJ 1941, p286)

Page 133 Tom Wilson with the Yoho Valley plaque at its unveiling. The plaque now marks his grave in the Old Banff Cemetery. (Whyte Museum of the Canadian Rockies, V701/LC-95)

Page 152 Rev. James Outram used Thompson Pass to access Mount Columbia, which he successfully climbed. (Whyte Museum of the Canadian Rockies, V14/AC 00P-80)

Page 154 Walter Wilcox (c), the first Caucasian to view the Alexandra valley, spent most of his life exploring in the Canadian Rockies. He is shown here with friends, outfitters Jim Brewster (l) and Tom Wilson (r). (Whyte Museum of the Canadian Rockies, V701/LC-90)

Page 155 C.S. Thompson (l) with fellow mountaineers (l–r): Charles Fey, unknown, Harold Dixon (seated), unknown, unknown, J. Norman Collie, Herschel Parker, and Peter Sarbach. (Whyte Museum of the Canadian Rockies, V653/NG-4-278)

Page 156 Mary Schäffer and Mollie Adams travelled extensively through the Rocky Mountains for three years until Mollie's untimely death in 1908. (Whyte Museum of the Canadian Rockies, V439/PS-4)

Page 159 Packer Sid Unwin assisted Mary Schäffer and Mollie Adams on their trips. (Whyte Museum of the Canadian Rockies, V527/PS-26)

Page 161 A.O. Wheeler, co-founder of the Alpine Club of Canada, learned mountain climbing as part of his profession. Many of his geological surveys had to be taken from high on a mountaintop. (Whyte Museum of the Canadian Rockies, NA71-970)

Page 162 Conrad Kain, highly regarded mountain climbing guide, often spent his winters trapping in remote parts of the Rocky Mountains. (Whyte Museum of the Canadian Rockies, V14/AC192-P/4)

Page 165 Jimmy Simpson with his pack train on the Saskatchewan Glacier. Simpson was the first outfitter to take his horses onto the ice. (Whyte Museum of the Canadian Rockies, V263/NA-71-6139)

Page 167 Caroline Hinman led her Off the Beaten Track tours throughout the Canadian Rockies. (Whyte Museum of the Canadian Rockies, NA 66-500)

Page 168 Byron Harmon travelled widely in the Canadian Rockies as part of his efforts to photograph all the major peaks. (Whyte Museum of the Canadian Rockies, V263/NA-71-4169)

Page 168 Lewis Freeman and his radio. Freeman was anxious to bring the world to visit every night while in the backcountry. (Whyte Museum of the Canadian Rockies, V263/NA-71-6331)

Page 170 Leopold Amery (r) politician, world traveller, and mountaineer with his friend, A.O. Wheeler, co-founder of the Alpine Club of Canada. (Whyte Museum of the Canadian Rockies, V14/AC 0P-634)

Page 170 Cliff and Ruth Kopas just before their 1933 marriage in Calgary. They left shortly thereafter to travel overland by horseback to the Pacific. (Courtesy of Keith Cole)

Back cover photo (Whyte Museum of the Canadian Rockies, V263/NA71-16)

All other photographs: Emerson Sanford

BIBLIOGRAPHY

Andrews, Gerry. "Beyond the Rugged Mountains." *Alberta History* 36:1 (1988).

Amery, L.C.M.S. *In the Rain and the Sun.* New York: Hutchinson, 1946.

Beers, Don. *Banff-Assiniboine: A Beautiful World.* Calgary: Highline Publishing, 1993.

Beers, Don. *The Wonder of Yoho: Scenes, Tales, Trails.* Calgary: Rocky Mountain Books, 1989.

Belliveau, Anne (McMullen). *Small Moments in Time: The Story of Alberta's Big West Country.* Calgary: Detselig Enterprises, 1999.

Berton, Pierre. *The National Dream: The Great Railway, 1871-1881.* Toronto: McClelland & Stewart, 1970.

Brennan, Brian. *Romancing the Rockies: Mountaineers, Missionaries, Marilyn and More.* Calgary: Fifth House, 2005.

Burns, Robert J. with Mike Schintz. *Guardians of the Wild: A History of the Warden Service of Canada's National Parks.* Calgary: University of Calgary Press, 2000.

"Canada's First Alpine Club Camp." *Canadian Alpine Journal* 1:1 (1907): 51.

Christensen, Lisa. *A Hiker's Guide to Art of the Canadian Rockies.* Calgary: Glenbow-Alberta Institute, 1996.

Cyndi Smith fonds. Whyte Museum of the Canadian Rockies, Banff, Alberta. M158.

Déziel-Letnick, Hélène, with E.J. Hart. *At Rest in the Peaks: A guided walk through the Old Banff Cemetery.* Banff: Whyte Museum of the Canadian Rockies, n.d.

Eaton, J.E.C. "An Expedition to the Freshfield Group." *Canadian Alpine Journal* 3 (1911): 1-13.

Edwards, Ralph. *The Trail to the Charmed Land.* Victoria: Herbert R. Larson, 1950.

Field, W. Osgood. "Mountaineering on the Columbia Icefield." *Appalachia* 16 (1924–76): 144.

Fraser, Esther. *Wheeler.* Banff: Summerthought, 1978.

Fraser, Esther. *The Canadian Rockies: Early Travels and Explorations.* Edmonton: Hurtig, 1969.

Freeman, Lewis R. *On the Roof of the Rockies.* Toronto: McClelland & Stewart, 1925.

"General Rides and Central Pow-Wow." *Trail Riders of the Canadian Rockies Bulletin* 1 (Oct. 15, 1924): 1.

Getty, Ian Allison Ludlow. *A Historical Guide to Yoho National Park.* Ottawa: Department of Indian Affairs and Northern Development, 1972.

Habel, Jean. "The North Fork of the Wapta." *Appalachia* 8 (1896–98): 328.

Haig, Bruce. *Following Historic Trails: James Hector, Explorer.* Calgary: Detselig Enterprises, 1983.

Hallworth, Beryl and Monica Jackson. *Pioneer Naturalists of the Rocky Mountains and the Selkirks.* Calgary: Calgary Field Naturalists Society, 1985.

Hammond Papers, Owens Art Gallery, Mount Allison University, Sackville, NB.

Hart, E.J. *Jimmy Simpson: Legend of the Rockies.* Canmore: Altitude Publishing, 1993.

Hart, E.J. *Ain't it Hell: Bill Peyto's "Mountain Journal."* Banff: EJH Literary Enterprises, 1995.

Henshaw, Julia W. "The Mountain Wildflowers of Western Canada." *Canadian Alpine Journal* 1:1 (1907): 130–37.

Hickson, J.W.A. "A Visit to the Saskatchewan Valley and Mount Forbes." *Canadian Alpine Journal* 12 (1922): 26–37.

Jenish, D'Arcy. *Epic Wanderer: David Thompson and the Mapping of the Canadian West.* Toronto: Doubleday Canada, 2003

Kain, Conrad. *Where the Clouds Can Go*, 3rd ed. Ed. with additional chapters by J. Monroe Thorington. New York: The American Alpine Club, 1979.

Kines, Gary Bret. *Chief Man-of-Many-Sides: John Murray Gibbon and his Contributions to the Development of Tourism and the Arts in Canada.* Ottawa: Carlton University, 2000.

Kopas, Cliff. *Packtrain to the Pacific.* Victoria: Touch Wood Editions, 2004.

Lillian Gest fonds. Whyte Museum of the Canadian Rockies. Banff, Alberta. M67.

Morton, Arthur S. *A History of the Canadian West to 1870-71*, 2nd ed. Edited by Lewis G. Thomas. Toronto: University of Toronto Press, 1973.

McCart, Joyce and Peter. *On the Road with David Thompson*. Calgary: Fifth House, 2000.

Nisbet, Jack. *Sources of the River: Tracking David Thompson across Western North America*. Seattle: Sasquatch Books, 1994.

Outram, James. *In the Heart of the Canadian Rockies*. New York: Macmillan, 1905.

Palliser, John. *The Papers of the Palliser Expedition, 1857-1860*. Edited, with introduction and notes by Irene M. Spry. Toronto: The Champlain Society, 1968.

Parker, Elizabeth. "In Memoriam: Edward Whymper." *Canadian Alpine Journal* 4 (1912): 126–36.

Patton, Brian and Bart Robinson. *The Canadian Rockies Trail Guide*, 7th ed. Banff: Summerthought, 2000.

Peter and Catherine Whyte Foundation, ed. *Great Days in the Rockies: The Photographs of Byron Harmon 1906-1934*. Banff: Altitude, 1984.

Russell, Bruce Hugh. "J. Singer Sargent in the Canadian Rockies." *The Beaver* 77:6 (Dec. 1997–Jan. 1998): 4–11.

Rylatt, R.M. *Surveying the Canadian Pacific: Memoir of a Railroad Pioneer*. Salt Lake City: University of Utah Press, 1991.

Sandford, Robert William. *Emerald Lake Lodge: A History and a Celebration*. Field: Canadian Rocky Mountain Resorts, 2002.

Sandford, R.W. *Yoho: A History and Celebration of Yoho National Park*. Canmore: Altitude, 1993.

Sanford, Emerson, and Janice Sanford Beck. *Life of the Trail 1: Historic Hikes in Eastern Banff National Park*. Calgary: Rocky Mountain Books, 2008.

Sanford Beck, Janice. *No Ordinary Woman: The Story of Mary Schäffer Warren*. Calgary: Rocky Mountain Books, 2001.

Schäffer, Mary T.S. "Old Indian Trails: Expedition of 1907." In *A Hunter of Peace: Mary T.S. Schäffer's Old Indian Trails of the Canadian Rockies*. Edited and annotated by E.J. Hart. Banff: The Whyte Foundation, 1980.

Schäffer, Mrs. Charles. *Untrodden Paths in the Canadian Rockies*. Minneapolis: Powers Mercantile Company, n.d.

Shadd, William and J. Monroe Thorington. "A Mountaineering Journey to the Columbia Icefield." *Canadian Alpine Journal* 14 (1924): 34–37.

Simpson, James. "Days Remembered." *American Alpine Journal* 19 (1974): 43–54.

Sleigh, Daphne. *Walter Moberly and the Northwest Passage by Rail*. Surrey, BC: Hancock House, 2003.

Smith, Cyndi. *Off the Beaten Track: Women Adventurers and Mountaineers in Western Canada*. Lake Louise: Coyote Books, 1989.

Solly, Godfrey A. "A Fortnight with the Canadian Alpine Club." *Canadian Alpine Journal* 2 (1910): 134–42.

Stanley, George F.G. "John Hammond: Painter for the CPR" In *The CPR West: The Iron Road and the Making of a Nation*. Edited by Hugh A. Dempsey. Vancouver: Douglas & McIntyre, 1984.

Stutfield, H.E.M., and J. Norman Collie. *Climbs and Exploration in the Canadian Rockies*. Calgary: Aquila Books, 1998.

Thorington, J. Monroe. "The Freshfield Group, 1922." *Canadian Alpine Journal* 13 (1923): 64–69.

Thorington, J. Monroe. *The Glittering Mountains of Canada*. Philadelphia: John W. Lea, 1925.

Vaux, George S. Jr. "The Wapta Fall." *Appalachia* 9 (1899–1901): 314.

Wade, Carson. *Human History of Yoho National Park*. Parks Canada, 1978.

Warrender, Susan. *"Mr. Banff:" The Story of Norman Luxton*. Calgary: Alistair Bear Enterprises, 2003.

Waterman, F.N. "From Field to Mount Robson – Summer 1923." *Canadian Alpine Journal* 14 (1924): 113–22.

Whyte, Jon. *Indians in the Rockies*. Banff: Altitude, 1985.

Wilcox, Walter D. "Bill Peyto." In *Tales from the Canadian Rockies*, edited by Brian Patton. (Edmonton: Hurtig Publishers, 1984.

Wilson, Thomas E. *Trailblazer of the Canadian Rockies*. Calgary: Glenbow-Alberta Institute, 1972.

Wilson, Tom. "Memories of Golden Days." *Canadian Alpine Journal* 14 (1924): 124–25.

Yochelson, Ellis L. *Smithsonian Institution Secretary: Charles Doolittle Walcott*. Ohio: Kent State University Press, 2001.

INDEX

Inter-provincial Boundary Survey   57, 160

James, Mary   109

Jordan, Glen   54

Kain, Conrad   160, 163, 167

Kananaskis   37, 85

Kananaskis Lakes   172, 200

Kaufmann, Christian   153

Kicking Horse Fire Road   70

Kicking Horse Pass   33, 37, 39, 40, 85, 86

Kicking Horse River   12, 50, 52, 58, 66, 70, 75, 79, 85, 91, 94, 97, 109, 140, 145

Kipling, Rudyard   96, 115

Kiwetinok Pass   53, 97, 106, 137, 146, 147

Kiwetinok River   52, 54, 147

Klucker   52, 53

Kootenay Indians   12, 24, 50, 85

Kootenay National Park   23, 132

Kootenay Plains   12, 23, 27, 28, 31, 32, 38, 44, 50, 53, 62, 64, 67, 163

Kootenay Trail   26, 57, 58

Kopas, Cliff   170, 172

Kopas, Ruth   170, 172

La Casse, Ulysses   164, 169

Ladd, Dr. William   164

La Gasse   24-26

Lake Louise (Laggan) Village   42, 45, 54, 56, 88, 94, 97, 101, 123, 134, 129, 164–166, 169

Lambe Creek   72

Laughing Falls   86, 92, 138, 142

Laut, Agnes   96

Leacock, Leonard   172

Le Blanc   24-26

Le Camble   27

Lewis and Clark   27

Lewis, Billy   160

Little Yoho River   53, 142, 147

Little Yoho Valley   53, 79, 104, 106, 107, 112, 116, 118, 135, 137, 138, 141, 142, 145-147

Lussier   27

Luxton, Norman   96

Lyell Glacier   33, 57

Lyell, Mount   33

Lyell, Sir Charles   33

Macoun, John   108

Maligne Lake   172

Martin, Tom   52, 106

Matterhorn   101-103

McArthur, J.J.   86, 107, 123, 137

McCorkell, Bert   54

McDonald, Finan   27, 29, 30

McGillivray, Duncan   24-26

McMaster   26

Meredith, Brian   171

Mistaya Canyon   63, 70, 71

Mistaya Lodge   17

Mistaya River   12, 33, 39, 49, 62, 70, 154, 160

Moberly, Walter   11, 37-40, 49

Mount Allison University   9, 97, 100

Nashan-esen   157, 158, 160

Natural Bridge   58, 70, 85, 90, 94, 131, 140

Nimrod   33

North Saskatchewan River   12, 23-25, 27, 33, 36, 40, 52, 57, 62, 64, 67, 70, 115, 153, 160, 166, 177-179

North West Company (Nor'Westers)   24-27

Off the Beaten Track   12, 58, 132, 151, 167

O'Hara, Lake   111, 116

Ottertail Fire Road   130

Otto, Bruce   54

Otto Creek   75

Outram, Rev. James   52, 53, 56, 108, 150, 153, 154, 157, 166

Outram's Shower Bath Falls   173, 180, 182

Padmore   85

Palliser, Captain John   33, 37

Palliser Expedition   11, 28, 33, 37

Palmer, Howard   54, 56

Parker, Elizabeth   109, 111, 112

Parker Ridge   165

Peigan   24, 27, 31, 32, 50

ABOUT THE AUTHORS

EMERSON SANFORD, originally from Nova Scotia, first visited the mountains of western Canada in the summer of 1961. Eleven years later, he moved to Alberta, and has been hiking ever since. After beginning to backpack seriously with his teenaged daughters in 1990, he began to wonder who cut the trails and how their routing had been determined. Since then, not only has he delved through printed material about the trails, he has also solo hiked every historic route and most long trails between Mount Robson and the Kananaskis Lakes – over 3000 km over five years! Emerson now lives in Canmore with his wife, Cheryl.

JANICE SANFORD BECK is the author of the best-selling *No Ordinary Woman: the Story of Mary Schäffer Warren* (Rocky Mountain Books, 2001). She has also written the introduction to the latest edition of Mary T.S. Schäffer's *Old Indian Trails of the Canadian Rockies* (Rocky Mountain Books, 2007) and, with Cheryl Sanford, researched the Mary Schäffer Warren portion of the Glenbow Museum's new permanent exhibit, Mavericks. Janice is presently masquerading as a flatlander, making her home in Saskatoon with her partner, Shawn, and their two children.

FURTHER READING ...

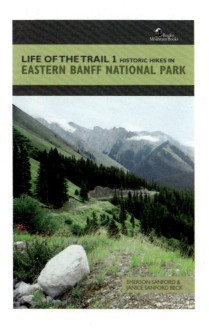

LIFE OF THE TRAIL 1

Historic Hikes in Eastern Banff National Park

Emerson Sanford & Janice Sanford Beck

Life of the Trail 1: Historic Hikes in Eastern Banff National Park follows the trails of David Thompson, Walter Wilcox, the Palliser Expedition, James Carnegie Earl of Southesk, Bill Peyto and A.P. Coleman. Along the way, the reader will journey from the Kootenay Plains to Lake Minnewanka, discovering the stories behind routes through the mountain towns of Banff and Lake Louise and along the Red Deer, Ptarmigan and Skoki valleys.

ISBN 978-1-894765-99-2

Colour Photos, Maps

$26.95, Softcover

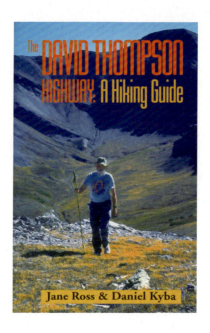

THE DAVID THOMPSON HIGHWAY
A Hiking Guide

Jane Ross & Daniel Kyba

This guide describes accessible hikes along Alberta's David Thompson Highway between Nordegg and Banff National Park. All 69 hikes start from the highway and range from walks of two hours to three-day journeys.

ISBN 978-0921102-70-0

B/W Photos, Maps

$16.95, Softcover

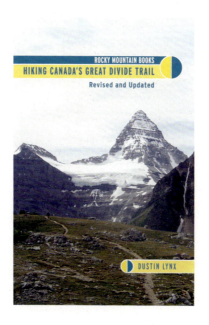

HIKING CANADA'S GREAT DIVIDE TRAIL
Revised & Updated

Dustin Lynx

Trekking the Continental Divide from the U.S. border to Kakwa Lake is a demanding adventure. In this revised and updated guidebook devoted to Canada's 1,200-kilometre Great Divide Trail (GDT), Dustin Lynx helps hikers piece together the myriad individual routes that form a continuous trail along the Divide. Lynx's indispensable pre-trip planning advice will help long-distance hikers overcome daunting logistical challenges such as resupply, navigation and access.

ISBN 978-1-894765-89-3

B/W Photos, Maps

$24.95, Softcover

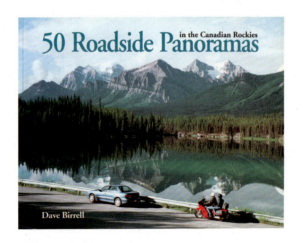

50 ROADSIDE PANORAMAS IN THE CANADIAN ROCKIES

Dave Birrell

Dave Birrell brings you 50 panoramas taken from highway viewpoints in the Canadian Rockies and the Eastern Slopes between Yellowhead Pass and Waterton. Photographs are accompanied by knowledgeable text, providing you with the fascinating stories behind the names of geographical features: mountains, passes, valleys and lakes.

ISBN 978-0921102-65-6

B/W Photos, Maps

$24.95, Softcover

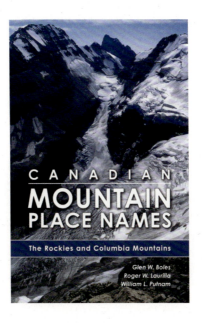

CANADIAN MOUNTAIN PLACE NAMES
The Rockies and Columbia Mountains

Glen W. Boles, Roger W. Laurilla, William L. Putnam

This is an entertaining and informative treatise on the toponymy of this increasingly popular alpine region, featuring the names of peaks, rivers, lakes and other geographic landmarks.

ISBN 978-1-894765-79-4

B/W Photos, Line Drawings

$19.95, Softcover

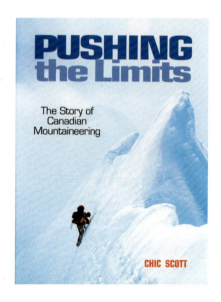

Pushing the Limits

The Story of Canadian Mountaineering

Chic Scott

Journeying to the summits, the crags and the gyms, from the west coast to Québec and from the Yukon to the Rockies, Chic introduces his readers to early mountain pioneers and modern-day climbing athletes.

ISBN 978-0921102-59-5

Colour & B/W Photos, Prints, Maps

$59.95, Hardcover

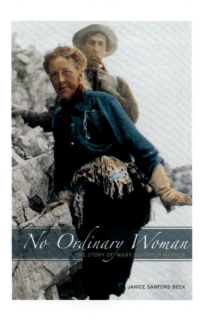

No Ordinary Woman

The Story of Mary Schäffer Warren

Janice Sanford Beck

Artist, photographer, writer, world traveller and, above all, explorer, Mary Schäffer Warren overcame the limited expectations of women at the turn of the 19th century in order to follow her dreams.

ISBN 978-0-921102-82-3
Colour & B/W Photos
$24.95, Paperback

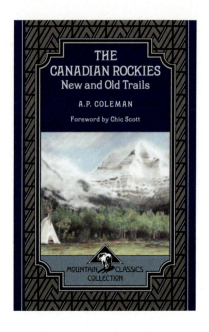

The Canadian Rockies: New and Old Trails
Mountain Classics Collection 1

A.P. Coleman
Foreword by Chic Scott

First published in 1911, this book gives modern-day readers a glimpse of the early days of mountaineering in the Canadian West. It paints a sympathetic picture of the rugged men and women who opened the region and of the hardships they endured.

ISBN 978-1894765-76-3

$19.95, Softcover

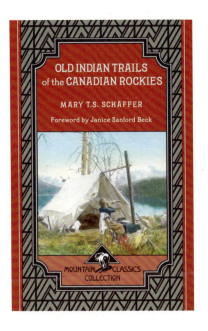

OLD INDIAN TRAILS OF THE CANADIAN ROCKIES
Mountain Classics Collection 2

Mary T.S. Schäffer
Foreword by Janice Sanford Beck

Mary T.S. Schäffer was an avid explorer and one of the first non-Native women to venture into the heart of the Canadian Rocky Mountains, where few women – or men – had gone before. First published in 1911, Old Indian Trails of the Canadian Rockies is Schäffer's story of her adventures in the traditionally male-dominated world of climbing and exploration.

ISBN 978-1-894765-77-0
$19.95 Softcover

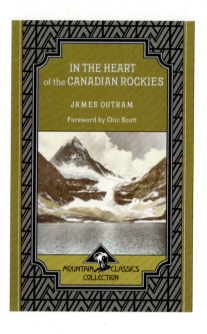

In the Heart of the Canadian Rockies
Mountain Classics Collection 3

James Outram
Foreword by Chic Scott

Born in 1864 in London, England, James Outram was a Church of England clergyman, mountaineer, author, businessman, militia officer and Orangeman who came to Canada at the turn of the 20th century after travelling and climbing throughout Europe. First published in 1905, In the *Heart of the Canadian Rockies* is Outram's record of his adventures and exploits in the early years of the 20th century among the massive mountains straddling the Alberta/British Columbia boundary.

ISBN 978-1-894765-96-1

$22.95, Softcover

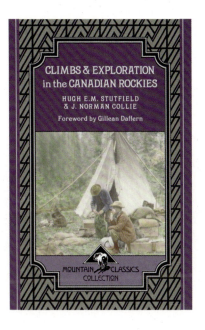

CLIMBS & EXPLORATION IN THE CANADIAN ROCKIES
Mountain Classics Collection 4

Hugh E.M. Stutfield & J. Norman Collie
Foreword by Gillean Daffern

First published in 1903, *Climbs & Exploration in the Canadian Rockies* details the mountaineering adventures of Hugh Stutfield and J. Norman Collie while the two were together during various explorations in the area north of Lake Louise, Alberta. Between 1898 and 1902, Stutfield and Collie journeyed through the mountain towns, valleys and passes of the Rockies, where Collie completed numerous first ascents and discovered fresh views of Lake Louise and the Columbia Icefields.

ISBN 978-1-897522-06-6

$22.95, Softcover

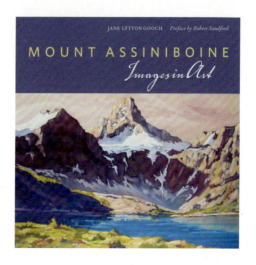

MOUNT ASSINIBOINE
Images in Art

Jane Lytton Gooch
Preface by Robert Sandford

Mount Assiniboine: Images in Art highlights a century of landscape art inspired by the Mount Assiniboine area of the Canadian Rockies from 1899 to 2006. The main text presents 42 colour plates illustrating a wide variety of styles and media from 23 artists including A.P. Coleman, Carl Rungius, James Simpson, Belmore Browne, Barbara and A.C. Leighton, Catharine and Peter Whyte, W.J. Phillips and A.Y. Jackson.

ISBN 978-1-894765-97-8
B/W & Colour Images
$29.95, Softcover